QUILTED FOR *Christmas*

BOOK III

Compiled by Barbara Weiland

Contributors

Leslie Beck · Joanne Case
Bob Coon · Melody Crust
Nancy Brenan Daniel
Bonnie Kaster
Michele O'Neil Kincaid
Mary Lynn Konyu
Virda Wilcox Lawrence
Susie Robbins · Lora Rocke
Heather W. Tewell · Retta Warehime
Tonee White · Johanna Wilson

❦ Credits ❦

Editorial Director .... Kerry I. Hoffman
Technical Editor .... Barbara Weiland
Copy Editor .... Liz McGehee
Proofreader .... Melissa Riesland
Illustrators .... Laurel Strand, Brian Metz, Carolyn Kraft

Design Director .... Judy Petry
Text and Cover Designer .... Sandy Wing
Production Assistant .... Shean Bemis
Photographer .... Brent Kane
Cover Background Quilt .... Roxanne Carter

That Patchwork Place®

Quilted for Christmas Book III
©1996 by That Patchwork Place, Inc.
PO Box 118, Bothell, WA 98041-0118 USA

Printed in Hong Kong
01 00 99 98 97 96   6 5 4 3 2 1

Quilted for Christmas, Book III / compiled by Barbara Weiland.
     p. cm.
   ISBN 1-56477-054-0 :
     1. Patchwork quilts. 2. Quilting—Patterns. 3. Appliqué. 4. Christmas decorations. I. Weiland, Barbara.
TT835.Q5357 1994
746.9'7—dc20
                                                        93-44135
                                                        CIP

This volume: ISBN 1-56477-143-1

Mission Statement

WE ARE DEDICATED TO PROVIDING QUALITY PRODUCTS
AND SERVICES THAT INSPIRE CREATIVITY.
WE WORK TOGETHER TO ENRICH THE LIVES WE TOUCH.

*That Patchwork Place is a
financially responsible ESOP company.*

Table of Contents

Introduction

Christmas is my favorite time of the year, perhaps because it brings back such vivid childhood memories—baking cookies with my sisters and brothers, helping Mom decorate the tree and wrap presents, singing Christmas carols with the family gathered around the piano, and keeping the Christmas secret alive for my youngest brother when the rest of us already knew Santa's identity.

Of all my cherished Christmas moments, the one that continues to bring me the most enjoyment year after year is making gifts for special friends and relatives. Stitching up small holiday quilts to give year 'round is a special opportunity to share my love of fabric and to give of my time. There's more than one quilt in this collection, the third in our *Quilted for Christmas* series, that will be on my gift-stitching list this year.

As the staff reviewed the entries and selected the best quilts to feature in this year's edition, we focused on smaller quilts—projects that wouldn't take lots of time or fabric to complete. That way, we knew you would be able to make several Christmas quilts to share with others this year. Of course, we selected a few larger, bed-size quilts for those of you who enjoy long-term projects—and we tried to include projects that would appeal to a wide range of skill levels.

In the pages that follow, you are sure to find a quilt or two that touches your heart right where Christmas resides. The designs of several nationally known quiltmakers, including Nancy Brenan Daniel, Retta Warehime, Leslie Beck, Susie Robbins, and Tonee White, as well as those from new designers and others who have contributed to past volumes are featured in the fifteen projects we've included for your stitching pleasure. Whether it's Santa, a beautiful angel, plum pudding, or glowing candles that conjure up holiday memories for you, you're sure to find just the right image to stitch in fabric for a special place in your home.

In addition to the quilts, we've included a wonderful Christmas stocking by Melody Crust, done in the Crazy-quilt style and embellished to the hilt. If you're looking for really quick quilted gifts, you'll love the group of potholders by Heather Tewell. Make them in holiday colors, or stitch up sets in the kitchen colors of the recipients.

There's something for everyone in this festive array of projects—appliqué, piecing, embroidery, and ribbon work are all represented. To make sure that you have everything you need to finish your project, we've also included a brief chapter on quiltmaking basics at the back of the book.

I hope you enjoy stitching these new Christmas treasures and pray that the spirit of Christmas surrounds you throughout the year as you make special holiday quilts to deck your own walls or to give as gifts to special friends and relatives.

Barbara Weiland

Poinsettia Wreath

By Joanne Case

Poinsettia Wreath by Joanne Case, 1994, Sultan, Washington, 32½" x 32½".

JOANNE CASE

JOANNE GREW UP IN WASHINGTON STATE AND ALASKA. THROUGHOUT HER LIFE, SHE HAS LOVED ALL FORMS OF NEEDLEWORK. SHE STARTED SEWING DOLL CLOTHES, DOING EMBROIDERY, AND CROCHETING WHEN SHE WAS JUST FIVE YEARS OLD. ONE OF HER FIRST MEMORIES OF QUILTING INCLUDES SITTING UNDER HER GRANDMOTHER'S QUILTING FRAME AND PUSHING NEEDLES UP THROUGH THE QUILT LAYERS TO THE WAITING FINGERS OF MEMBERS OF THE LADIES AID SOCIETY. THEY WERE MAKING QUILTS FOR THE RED CROSS DURING WORLD WAR II.

THIRTEEN YEARS AGO, QUILTING BECAME JOANNE'S MAIN NEEDLE-ART INTEREST WHEN SHE AND HER DAUGHTER TOOK A QUILT CLASS TOGETHER. WITHIN A YEAR, SHE HAD BECOME AN ACTIVE MEMBER OF THE BUSY BEE QUILTERS IN SNOHOMISH, WASHINGTON.

IN 1989, JOANNE ESTABLISHED THE BUSY BEES' ANNUAL DOLL-QUILT PROJECT. THE RESULTING QUILTS ARE CONTRIBUTED TO THE SALVATION ARMY FOR DISTRIBUTION TO FAMILIES IN NEED AT CHRISTMAS. EACH OF THE QUILTS ACCOMPANIES A DOLL DRESSED WITH HANDMADE AND PURCHASED WARDROBES, DONATED BY THE GTE NORTHWEST EMPLOYEES, FAMILIES, AND RETIRED PERSONNEL.

JOANNE LOVES TRADITIONAL AND CONTEMPORARY QUILTS AND TEACHES BOTH TYPES OF QUILTMAKING. SHE HAS RECEIVED NUMEROUS AWARDS FOR HER QUILTS—MOST OF WHICH ARE HER OWN DESIGNS. SHE HOPES TO MARKET PATTERNS FOR SOME OF THEM IN THE FUTURE.

JOANNE IS MARRIED AND HAS FIVE CHILDREN AND NINE GRANDCHILDREN.

IF YOU'RE FAMILIAR WITH THE BEAUTIFUL AND POPULAR WATERCOLOR QUILTS, YOU'RE ONE STEP AHEAD WITH THIS PROJECT. YOU FOLLOW THE SAME DESIGN PRINCIPLES, BUT YOU NEED ONLY TWO FABRICS INSTEAD OF HUNDREDS! THIS WREATH IS ONE IN A SERIES JOANNE CALLS "TWO-FABRIC WATERCOLOR QUILTS." ALTHOUGH POINSETTIAS REMIND US OF WINTER HOLIDAYS, THE COLORS IN THIS WREATH ARE APPROPRIATE YEAR 'ROUND.

Quilt Size: 32½ x 32½

Materials: 42"-wide fabric

(Medium- to large-scale print is recommended.)

1 yd. poinsettia or other floral print for the wreath

1 yd. light print or stripe for the background squares and outer border

3" squares of paper-backed fusible web

1 yd. for backing

½ yd. coordinating solid for the inner border and binding

36" x 36" piece of low-loft batting

Metallic or rayon embroidery thread for embellishing and quilting

Cutting

Cut all strips across the width (crosswise grain) of the fabric.

From the wreath fabric, cut:
8 strips, each 3" x 42"; crosscut into 3" squares
(You may need to cut additonal strips and squares.)

From the light fabric, cut:
6 strips, each 3" x 42"; crosscut into 3" squares
4 strips, each 1¾" x 42", for the outer border

From the inner border fabric, cut:
4 strips, each 1½"x 42", for the inner border
4 strips, each 2" x 42", for the binding

Arranging the Squares

For the best results, work on a design wall—a piece of flannel, fleece, or batting attached to the wall in an area where you can stand back to evaluate your work.

1. Following the diagram below, arrange the squares for each of the 11 rows. As you place the squares on the design wall, work to build a roughly circular shape for the wreath.

2. Stand back and evaluate what you have created. Referring to the quilt photo, rearrange the floral pieces to create a pleasing arrangement of flowers and leaves. You may need to discard some squares and cut new ones from the remaining fabric.

   Twist, turn, and move the squares around until you're happy with the results. Work toward blending the design and color and eliminating any abrupt changes from square to square. Use a reducing glass or squint to evaluate your work and detect areas that require attention. Use the wrong side of the fabric in some areas to produce subtle shading.

Softening the Edges

When you are satisfied with your composition, soften the inner and outer edges of the wreath by extending the leaves and flowers to look more natural. To do so, "fussy cut" partial squares to complete the flowers and leaves that end abruptly where the wreath and background fabrics meet.

"Fussy cut" applied to background square

1. Look through the leftover squares of wreath fabric for just the right shapes.
2. Apply paper-backed fusible web to the wrong side of the selected squares.

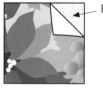

Fusible web

3. From these squares, cut out the floral and leaf shapes that will soften the hard edges of the wreath.

4. Remove the paper backing from each shape and position where desired on the background squares. Fuse in place, following the manufacturer's directions. Return the fused squares to their position in the quilt layout.

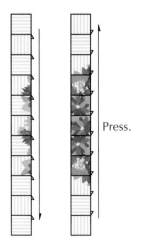

Outline of wreath (lower left corner)

Edge-softening "fussy cuts"

Background fabric

Wreath fabric

Assembling the Quilt Top

1. Before you begin, mark the top of each square with a pin to help keep them in correct order. Sew the squares together in vertical rows. Press the seams in opposite directions from row to row.

Press.

2. Sew the rows together, carefully matching the seams between the squares. Press all joining seams in one direction.
3. Sew each inner border strip to an outer border strip. Press the seam toward the darker fabric in each strip unit.

Outer border ——▶

Inner border ——▶

4. Attach the borders, following the directions for "Borders with Mitered Corners" on page 125.

Embellishing

1. Set your machine for a narrow satin stitch and thread it with metallic or rayon embroidery thread.
2. Satin-stitch over the raw edges of the fused pieces. Test the stitch on scraps first, adjusting the stitching so the bobbin thread does not show on the surface and the fabric doesn't pucker. To prevent puckering, add stabilizer to the wrong side and place the work in an embroidery hoop.
3. Add a few satin-stitched tendrils to extend the design onto the background squares.

Tendrils extend onto background squares.

Finishing

Refer to pages 124–28 to finish your quilt.

1. Mark the quilt top with the desired quilting pattern or follow the quilting suggestion below.
2. Layer the quilt top with batting and backing; baste.
3. Quilt on the marked lines in the background, using a decorative thread if desired.
4. With the feed dogs lowered and the darning foot or open-toe embroidery foot attached, free-motion quilt around the flowers and leaves. Stop when you have added enough glitter.
5. Attach a hanging sleeve if desired.
6. Bind the edges with double-fold binding, using 2½"-wide bias or straight-grain strips cut from the coordinating solid.
7. Sign your quilt.

Heart's Delight

By Susie Robbins

Heart's Delight *by Susie Robbins, 1995, Danville, California, 34" x 34".*

SUSIE ROBBINS

SUSIE IS THE EXUBERANT DESIGNER OF WONDERFUL DOLL PATTERNS THAT SHE MARKETS THROUGH HER COMPANY, PEDDLERS OF DANVILLE. SHE STARTED MAKING QUILTS TEN YEARS AGO. NATURALLY ATTRACTED TO THE FABRICS SURROUNDING HER IN THE QUILT SHOP WHERE SHE WORKED AT THE TIME, SUSIE SAYS SHE "TRIED DESPERATELY NOT TO GET HOOKED" ON QUILTMAKING. THE FIRST CLASS SUSIE TOOK—ON FEATHERED STAR QUILTS—WAS A CHALLENGE, BUT SHE KEPT ON TAKING CLASSES FROM TEACHERS LIKE SHARYN CRAIG, WHO INSPIRED HER TO "GO FEARLESSLY INTO THE QUILT WORLD." SHE NOW BLENDS HER TWO LOVES AND HAS TRIED HER HAND AT DESIGNING QUILT FABRICS AS WELL.

SUSIE ORIGINALLY DESIGNED "HEART'S DELIGHT" AS A FULL-SIZE BED QUILT FOR HER DAUGHTER, BECKY. IT WAS A GRADUATION GIFT IN THE COLORS OF THE UNIVERSITY WHERE BECKY WAS HEADED. SINCE THIS TYPE OF QUILT HAD BECOME A FAMILY TRADITION, SUSIE WASN'T SURPRISED WHEN BECKY APPEARED ONE DAY WITH A DRAWING AND SAID, "THIS IS MY DESIGN FOR MY GRADUATION QUILT." SUSIE COULDN'T REFUSE BECKY A QUILT OF STARS SET IN SASHING WITH AN APPLIQUÉD BORDER AND NOT A HEART TO BE SEEN. SO, SHE SET ASIDE THE HEARTS TEMPORARILY. SHE LATER RESCUED SOME OF THE BLOCKS FROM THE FIRST QUILT TO CREATE THIS CHEERFUL WALL HANGING, THEN EMBELLISHED IT TO HER "HEART'S DELIGHT" WITH RIBBONS, ROSES, AND BEADS.

Quilt Size: 34" x 34"

Materials: 44"-wide fabric

5 strips of assorted Christmas prints, each 1³/₄" x 42", for scrappy pieced blocks* or ¼ yd. of 1 Christmas print for identical pieced blocks

³/₈ yd. white-on-white print #1 for pieced-block backgrounds

³/₈ yd. white-on-white print #2 for large appliqué-block backgrounds

Assorted Christmas plaids and prints for small heart block backgrounds and hearts**

¼ yd. red poinsettia print for large hearts and some small hearts

1¹/₈ yds. fabric for backing

36" x 36" piece of batting

10 to 12 strips, each 1¹/₄" x 42", cut from assorted Christmas prints for pieced bias binding

Scraps of Christmas prints for binding

*Use at least 3 different prints or use 1 strip each of 5 different prints.

**If you are using scraps, they should be no smaller than 3¹/₂" square. Include some prints with white backgrounds. Fat-quarter packets of Christmas prints are a nice alternative to scraps.

Embellishments

Assorted red ribbons in various widths

Small gold and pearl beads

Assorted small gold heart charms and gold star sequins

Gold metallic thread

Silk ribbon for embroidery

Cutting

Use the heart templates on page 16.

1. For scrappy blocks, cut each of the 5 Christmas-print strips 1¾" x 32". For identical blocks, cut 3 strips, each 1¾" x 42", from the ¼ yd. of Christmas print.

2. For scrappy blocks, cut 5 strips, each 1¾" x 32", from the white-on-white fabric for pieced blocks. For identical blocks, cut 4 strips, each 1¾" x 32".

3. From white-on-white print #2, cut 4 squares, each 9" x 9", for the large heart appliqué blocks.

4. From the poinsettia print, cut 4 large hearts for appliqué (method of your choice on pages 121–23).

5. From the assorted plaids and prints, cut:
   28 squares, each 4½" x 4½", for the border blocks
   5 squares, each 4" x 4", for pieced block centers
   33 small hearts for appliqué (method of your choice)

Assembling the Blocks

1. Sew each of the Christmas-print strips to a white-on-white strip of background fabric. Press the seam toward the Christmas-print strip in each pair. The finished strip pairs should measure 3" wide.

2. If you are making scrappy blocks, cut 8 segments, each 1¾" wide, and 4 segments, each 4" wide, from

each of the 5 strip pairs. For identical blocks, cut 40 segments, each 1¾" wide, and 20 segments, each 4" wide, from the strip pairs.

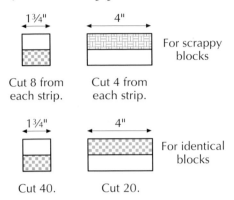

| For scrappy blocks |
| For identical blocks |

3. Arrange the segments with the 4" center squares to form 5 pieced blocks. For scrappy blocks, play with color placement in the four-patch units.

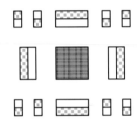

4. When you are satisfied with the arrangement of the pieces for each block, assemble the four-patch units and return them to their positions in each block arrangement.

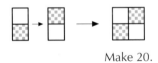

Make 20.

5. Sew the pieces for each block together in rows, then sew the rows together, pressing as directed by the arrows.

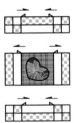

6. Appliqué a small heart to the center square in each pieced block. Choose a color that contrasts with the square. Appliqué a large heart in the center of each white-on-white background square.

Make 4.   Make 5.

7. Arrange the pieced and appliquéd blocks in 3 rows of 3 blocks each. Sew the blocks together in rows, pressing the seams toward the appliqué blocks. Sew the rows together.

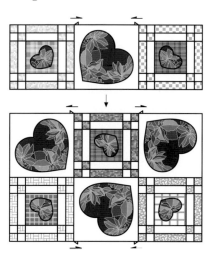

8. Working on a large, flat surface or a design wall, arrange the 4¾" border squares around the quilt-top center in a pleasing arrangement, then position hearts in the blocks. Play with the placement until you are happy with the results. Appliqué each heart to its square.

9. Sew the heart blocks together to make the borders as shown. Press the seams toward the darker squares.

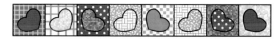

Make 2.

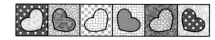

Make 2.

10. Sew the short border strips to opposite sides of the quilt top. Press the seams toward the border strips. Sew the long borders to the remaining quilt-top edges; press.

Finishing

Refer to pages 124–28 to finish your quilt.

1. Mark the quilt top with the desired quilting patterns or follow the quilting suggestion below.

 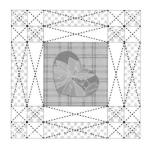

Appliqué Block   Pieced Block

2. Layer the quilt top with batting and backing; baste.
3. Quilt on the marked lines.
4. Embellish the hearts as desired, referring to "Embellishing" on page 14 and "Ribbon Roses" on page 15.
5. Add a hanging sleeve if desired.
6. Bind the quilt, using pieced bias binding made as shown in the box on page 14.
7. Sign your quilt.

Pieced Bias Binding

1. Arrange the 1¼" x 42" Christmas-print strips in a pleasing order. Sew them together, forming 1 strip unit, and press all the seams in one direction.

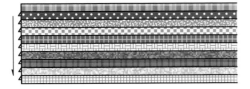

2. Cut the strip unit in half crosswise and sew the 2 pieces together.

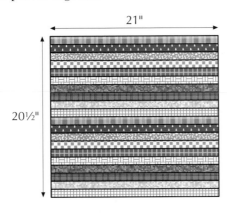

3. Cut 1½"-wide true bias strips from the pieced square.

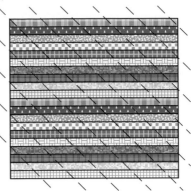

Cut 1½"-wide bias strips.

4. Sew the strips together to make a continuous piece, 4½ yds. long.
5. Turn under ¼" at one end of the binding and press. Stitch the single-layer binding to the quilt, using a ³⁄₈"-wide seam allowance and mitering the corners as shown for double-fold binding on page 128. Turn the binding to the inside, turning under the raw edge along the stitching line. Hand sew in place.

Turn under ¼" at one end.

Embellishing

If you love handwork and "gilding the lily," you will have fun embellishing to your heart's delight. Refer to the quilt photo for ideas.

1. Following the guide at right, embellish each large heart with 3 ribbon roses and 2 or more bows. Loop and tack the bow tails with a few stitches. (See "Ribbon Roses," page 15.)
2. Add beads, gold metallic quilting stitches, charms, and sequins as desired.
3. Add simple bows, beads, and stitchery to the small hearts in the pieced blocks and to all or some of the border hearts as desired.

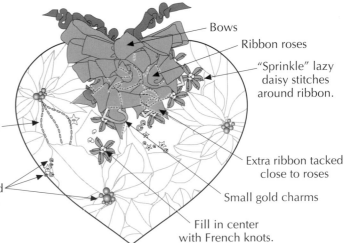

Bows

Ribbon roses

"Sprinkle" lazy daisy stitches around ribbon.

Embellish fabric design with metallic gold thread and quilting stitches.

Extra ribbon tacked close to roses

Accent fabric design with gold and glass-bead star sequins.

Small gold charms

Fill in center with French knots.

Ribbon Roses

1. Cut an 8"- to 10"-long piece of 1"-wide ribbon and fold it in half at a 45° angle.

2. Fold the upper ribbon tail (A) back over the straight edge of the first fold and hold firmly in place.

Dashed line is the diagonal fold underneath.

3. Fold the lower tail (B) up against the straight edge of the ribbon and hold in place.

4. Fold the lower tail (A) back against the ribbon edge. Notice that the folds have created a "square" on the top side, and a square divided in half on the underside.

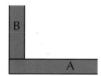

5. Continue folding the tails in this manner until you have used up most of the ribbon. Then, holding the two tails in one hand, let go of the folded ribbon; it will pop up into a column of folds.

6. Gently tug on one of the tails to pull the folds into a rose and tack all layers together with 2 or 3 small stitches. Finish on the back with a few stitches. Do not trim the ribbon tails. Stitch in place but do not cut the thread. Leave it attached so you can use it later to attach the finished rose to the quilt top.

7. Position the roses as desired on the large appliquéd hearts—several roses nestled together is nice. Hand tack the roses in place and add a bead or cluster of small beads to the center if desired. Bunch the ribbon tails in small loops and tack in place, adding beads if desired.

Appliqué Templates

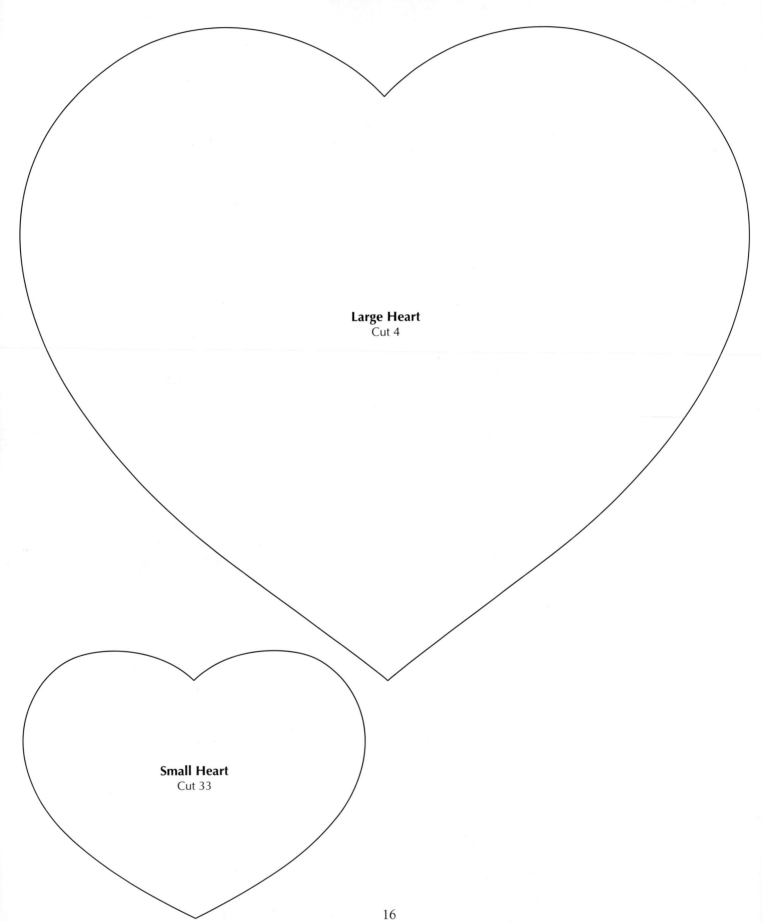

Large Heart
Cut 4

Small Heart
Cut 33

Cranberry Relish

By Bob Coon

Cranberry Relish by Bob Coon, 1994, Tacoma, Washington, 38" x 49".

BOB COON

BOB COMES FROM A LONG LINE OF QUILTERS. HIS MOTHER, ROSE MARIE, IS ALSO A QUILTER. AT THE FAMILY FARM IN SOUTHWESTERN OKLAHOMA, BOB'S GRANDMOTHER WALD OFTEN HAD A QUILT ON A FRAME IN FRONT OF THE PICTURE WINDOW SO FRIENDS COULD SEE IT ON THEIR WAY TO TOWN. BOB OWNS AND CHERISHES SEVERAL QUILTS MADE BY HIS GRAND-MOTHER AND GREAT-GRANDMOTHER.

AT THE AGE OF TWELVE, BOB BEGAN DOING A VARIETY OF NEEDLE ARTS. HE GOT HIS FIRST SEWING MACHINE IN DECEMBER 1977 AND IT HAS BEEN GOING EVER SINCE.

BOB'S TEACHING CAREER BEGAN IN TACOMA, WASH-INGTON, IN 1989. TODAY HE TEACHES AT QUILT SHOPS IN THE PACIFIC NORTHWEST AND NATIONALLY AT SEMINARS AND QUILT GUILDS. HE HAS DEVELOPED A REPUTATION FOR ACCURACY, CREATIVITY, AND INNOVATION.

WHETHER WORKING WITH TRADITIONAL DESIGNS OR CREATING ORIGINALS, BOB LOOKS FOR WAYS TO SIMPLIFY TECHNIQUES: "THE EASIER IT IS FOR ME TO DO, THE EASIER IT IS FOR MY STUDENTS."

BOB HAS ALWAYS BEEN FASCINATED WITH PICKLE DISH WEDDING RING QUILTS, AND MAKING ONE OF HIS OWN HAS BEEN A LONGTIME GOAL. HE BEGAN EXPERIMENT-ING WITH THE DESIGN, USING FOUNDATION PIECING, AND DISCOVERED IT TO BE THE IDEAL METHOD FOR CREATING CONSISTENT, NEAR-PERFECT ARCS.

CRANBERRY GOES WITH CHRISTMAS, SO BOB CHOSE A "RELISH" RED, DEEP EVER-GREEN, AND SOFT WHITE TO ESTABLISH A MOOD OF CHRISTMAS PAST. BOB IS KNOWN FOR HIS WORK IN SOLIDS—HE LOVES THE GRAPHIC LOOK THEY CONVEY—AND WHEN HE USES PRINTS, HE USUALLY CHOOSES DESIGNS THAT "READ" AS SOLIDS, ONES WITH SUBTLE TEXTURE LIKE THE FABRICS IN THIS QUILT.

A LARGER CRANBERRY RELISH QUILT IS IN THE WORKS, FULFILLING BOB'S WISH FOR A FULL-SIZE VERSION OF THIS CLASSIC PATTERN.

Quilt Size: 38" x 49"

Materials: 44"-wide fabric

2½ yds. red miniprint for arcs

2½ yds. green miniprint for arcs and binding

1 yd. white print for background

1½ yds. for backing

42" x 54" piece of thin batting

Tracing paper or plain newsprint

Cutting

Use templates on pages 22–23.

From the red miniprint, cut:
25 strips, each 2" x 42", for the arcs*
62 of Template B
31 of Template C

From the green miniprint, cut:
29 strips, each 2" x 42", for the arcs*

From the white print, cut:
12 of Template D

*The number of strips will vary depending on how efficiently you piece the arcs.

Piecing the Arcs

When you piece the arcs, you will always sew with the paper foundation piece right side up on top of your fabric strips.

1. Trace 62 of Template A for the paper arcs, making sure you trace *all* the lines. (Photocopying can distort the shape enough to affect the piecing. If you wish to use a photocopy machine, first test it carefully for accuracy.) Cut out each piece A on the outer lines.

2. Lay a green strip on top of a red strip, right sides together and raw edges aligned. Lay a paper arc *with stitching lines face up* on the strips as shown, with the first stitching line approximately 1/4" from the raw edges. Sew on the line, using a short stitch (1.5mm European or 16 stitches/inch American).

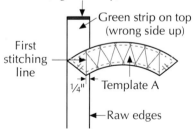

Red strip underneath
(right side up)

Green strip on top
(wrong side up)

First
stitching
line

1/4"

Template A

Raw edges

3. Add additional paper arcs to the strips, leaving no more than 1/8" between arcs. Sew. Press the seam toward the red strip.

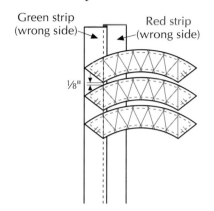

Green strip
(wrong side)

Red strip
(wrong side)

1/8"

Carefully cut the arcs apart and trim the excess fabric at the edges of each arc. (Be sure to press each seam before you cut the arcs apart or trim the excess fabric.)

4. Lay a trimmed arc on the right side of a green strip as shown, with the second stitching line approximately 1/4" from the raw edge of the green strip. Sew on the line. Stitch additional arcs to the green strip as in step 3.

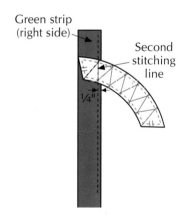

Green strip
(right side)

Second
stitching
line

1/4"

Press the seam toward the green strip; cut the arcs apart and trim. Trim the excess red fabric between the paper arc and the green strip flush with the green seam allowance.

5. Continue adding wedges by stitching the arcs to the strips, alternating red and green, until you have sewn on all the stitching lines. Make a total of 62 red-and-green arcs. On each arc, transfer the hash marks from Template A to the fabric.

6. Carefully remove the paper foundation. Try not to pull on the fabric because the arcs distort easily. Instead, gently tear the paper away from the stitching lines.

Assembling the Units

1. Divide the arcs into 2 groups of 31 each. Add a piece B to each end of the arcs in the first group, matching the hash marks. Press the seams toward the B pieces. Make a total of 31 units. Fold each arc in half; mark the midpoint on the inside curve.

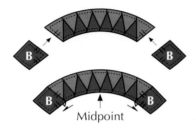

Make 31.

2. Fold a piece C in half and mark the midpoint on each curve. Fold an arc from the second group (without the B pieces) in half and mark the midpoint on the inside curve. With right sides together and the arc on top, match the midpoints and pin the arc and piece C together. Stitch. Press the seam toward piece C. Make a total of 31 units.

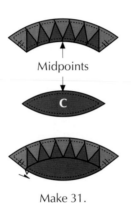

Midpoints

Make 31.

3. Pin a unit made in step 1 to a unit made in step 2, matching the midpoints on the curves. Also match each point 1/4" from the raw edge on the A/B seam with each point 1/4" from the raw edge on the A/C seam. Pin the remainder of the edges. Stitch to complete 1 "football." Press the seam toward piece C. Make a total of 31 footballs.

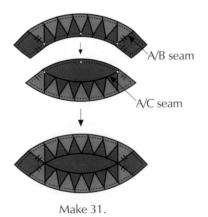

A/B seam

A/C seam

Make 31.

4. Mark the midpoint on each curve of a football and a piece D. With right sides together and the football on top, match the midpoints on the curves; pin. Match the point 1/4" from the raw edge on the football A/B seam with the point at one tip of piece D; pin. Repeat at the other end of the football. Beginning at one pin, sew a few stitches; backstitch. Sew to the other pin; backstitch. Do not press the seam yet.

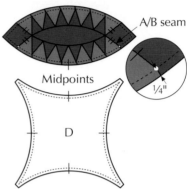

A/B seam

Midpoints

1/4"

D

5. Add 3 more footballs to piece D in the same manner to complete Unit 1. *Press the football/D seams toward the footballs* to create dimension on the quilt top. Do not sew the piece B seams together yet.

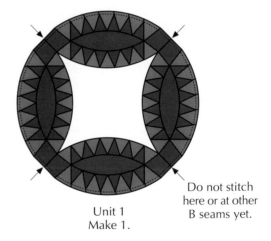

Unit 1
Make 1.

Do not stitch here or at other B seams yet.

6. Make 5 units with 3 footballs each (Unit 2) and 6 units with 2 footballs each (Unit 3) as shown. Press the seams as before. Do not sew the piece B seams.

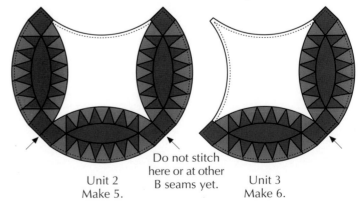

Do not stitch here or at other B seams yet.

Unit 2
Make 5.

Unit 3
Make 6.

Assembling the Quilt Top

1. Sew the units together in 4 rows as shown. Press the seams as before. Do not sew the piece B seams together yet.

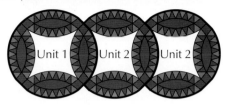

Make 1 row.

Make 3 rows.

2. Sew the rows together, sewing the piece B seams together and pressing seams in opposite directions.

Finishing

Refer to pages 124–28 to finish your quilt.

1. Layer the quilt top with batting and backing; baste.
2. Quilt as desired or follow the quilting suggestion shown below.

3. Trim the excess batting and backing even with the scalloped quilt-top edge.
4. Add a hanging sleeve if desired.
5. Bind the edges, following the directions for "Binding Scalloped Edges" in the sidebar at right.
6. Sign your quilt.

Binding Scalloped Edges

Attaching the binding on a scalloped edge requires two steps: sewing the binding around the curve and turning an inside corner.

1. To prepare the double-fold binding, follow the directions on pages 127–28, with this important change: *cut the bias strips 1³/₄" wide.* Prepare enough binding to go around the perimeter of the quilt, adding an extra 15" total for the inside corners.
2. Beginning at the outer edge of a curve, pin the binding around the curve. Be careful not to stretch the binding. Using a ¹/₄"-wide seam allowance, start stitching about 1" from the beginning of the binding. Continue stitching around the curve, stopping at the point where the stitching lines would intersect, below the **V** of the scallop. Backstitch.

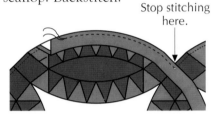

Stop stitching here.

3. Remove the quilt from the machine. Pin the binding to the adjoining curve. As the binding turns the inside corner, a small fold will form. Begin stitching in the spot where you ended on the previous curve; backstitch. Continue around the scalloped edge of the quilt.

Start stitching at same spot where previous stitching ended.

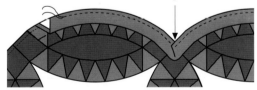

4. Fold the binding to the back of the quilt, turning one scallop at a time. A folded miter will form at the inside corners. Blindstitch the binding to the back of the quilt. The folded miter may also be closed with a blind stitch.

Piecing and Quilting Templates

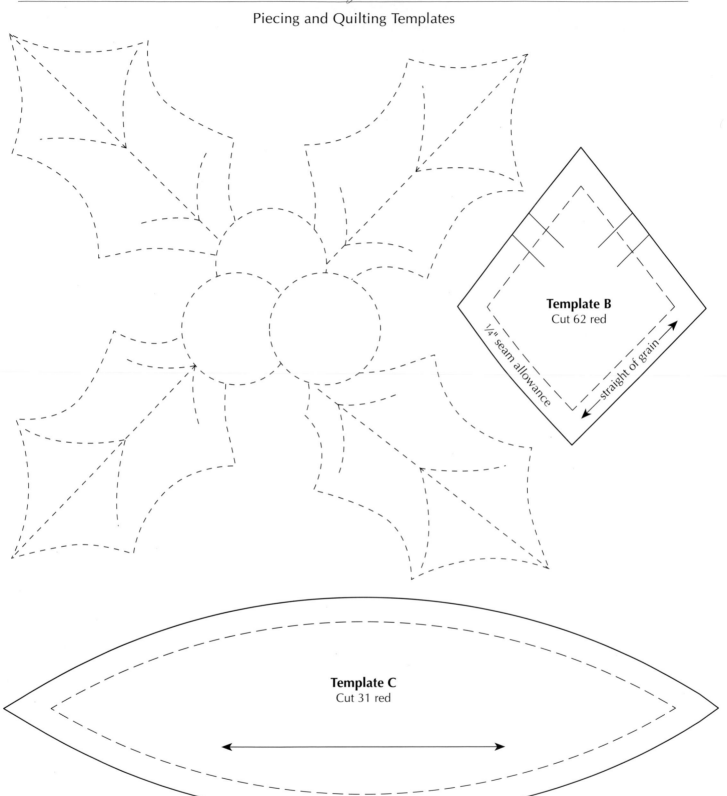

Template B
Cut 62 red

¼" seam allowance

straight of grain

Template C
Cut 31 red

Piecing Templates

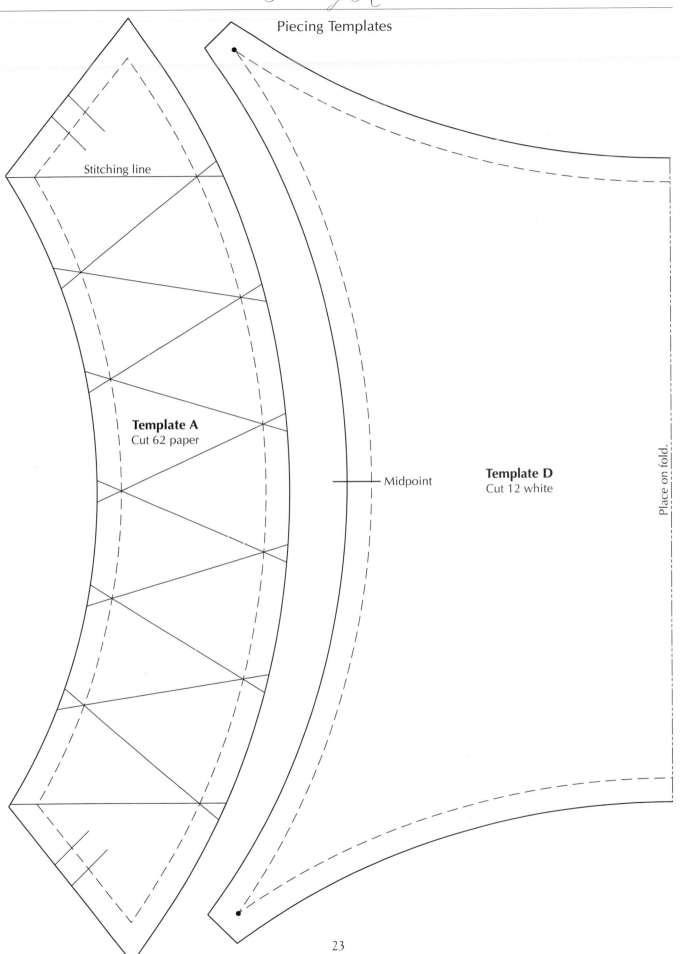

Stitching line

Template A
Cut 62 paper

— Midpoint

Template D
Cut 12 white

Place on fold.

23

Poinsettia Christmas Quilt

By Nancy Brenan Daniel

Poinsettia Christmas Quilt *by Nancy Brenan Daniel, 1995, Tempe, Arizona, 78$\frac{1}{2}$" x 96$\frac{1}{2}$".*

NANCY BRENAN DANIEL

NANCY HAS BEEN A TEACHER SINCE 1965 AND HAS BEEN TEACHING QUILTING AND DOLLMAKING SINCE 1971. SHE IS DEDICATED TO TEACHING NEEDLE ARTS AS POSITIVE AVENUES FOR CREATIVE EXPRESSION.

NANCY COMES BY HER LOVE OF QUILTING NATURALLY. HER GRANDMOTHER, MARY TALKINGTON RITZENTHALER, WAS A LIFELONG QUILTER, AND NANCY'S MOTHER, MARY E. R. BRENAN, FINISHED HER FIRST QUILT AT AGE SEVENTY-FIVE AND HER SECOND WHEN SHE WAS EIGHTY-TWO!

NANCY HOLDS BACHELOR'S AND MASTER'S DEGREES IN FINE ARTS WITH AN EMPHASIS IN ART HISTORY. SHE WRITES AND DESIGNS FOR SEWING-RELATED PUBLICATIONS, INCLUDING HER OWN SMALL PATTERN COMPANY, LOVE TOKEN PATTERNS. HER QUILTS, GARMENTS, AND DOLLS ARE OFTEN EXHIBITED IN GALLERIES, MUSEUMS, AND PRIVATE COLLECTIONS.

NANCY LIVES IN THE ARIZONA DESERT WITH HER HUSBAND, NORM, A UNIVERSITY PROFESSOR. THEY HAVE THREE ADULT CHILDREN: KAREN, DAVID, AND STEPHEN. THEIR PERMANENT COMPANIONS ARE CATS INKY JOSEPH AND ELKY JANE AND DOG TOBY. NANCY IS AN AVID GARDENER OF IRIS BULBS AND FRUIT TREES.

THE "POINSETTIA CHRISTMAS QUILT" IS A DESIGN FOR THE DETERMINED FABRIC COLLECTOR—A DIFFERENT RED FABRIC WAS USED IN EACH OF THE SIXTY-THREE BLOCKS. THERE ARE MORE THAN ONE HUNDRED FABRICS IN THIS SCRAPPY QUILT. MOST OF THE FABRICS ARE NOT HOLIDAY PRINTS. THE OVERALL EFFECT IS THAT THE QUILT WAS MADE FROM A COLLECTION OF ANTIQUE BLOCKS.

NANCY DESIGNED THE POINSETTIA BLOCK SPECIFICALLY FOR QUILT-GUILD CHRISTMAS BLOCK EXCHANGES AND DRAWINGS. FOR NANCY, EACH BLOCK IN A FRIENDSHIP QUILT REPRESENTS THE SPECIAL QUALITIES OF THE MEMBER WHO MADE IT. AS THE MEMBERS REACH OUT TO EACH OTHER, THEY ARE NURTURED—IN A NEVER-ENDING CHAIN OF FRIENDSHIP.

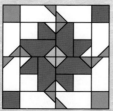

Poinsettia Block

Quilt Size: 78½" x 96½"

Materials: 44"-wide fabric (or scraps)

2 yds. total assorted red prints for poinsettias and corner squares

1½ yds. total assorted green prints for leaves and corner squares

⅜ yd. total assorted yellow prints for poinsettia centers

3½ yds. total assorted beige prints for background

½ yd. green print for inner border

2 yds. red-and-green floral print for outer border and binding

5¼ yds. for backing

82½" x 100½" piece of batting

Cutting for One Block*

From the red prints, cut:
    4 rectangles, each 2" x 3½"
    1 strip, 2" x 8½"
    2 squares, each 2" x 2"
From the green prints, cut:
    2 squares, each 2" x 2"
    12 squares, each 1½" x 1½"
From the beige prints, cut:
    8 rectangles, each 2" x 3½"
    4 squares, each 1½" x 1½"
    1 strip, 2" x 8½"
From the yellow prints, cut:
    4 squares, each 1½" x 1½"

*To make the quilt in the size shown, make 63 blocks.

Piecing the Poinsettia Block

To make each block:

1. Draw a diagonal line on the wrong side of each green, beige, and yellow 1½" square.

2. Sew the 2" x 8½" beige strip to the 2" x 8½" red strip. Press the seam toward the red strip. Crosscut the strip unit into 4 segments, each 2" wide.

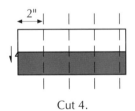

Cut 4.

3. Position a beige square face down on the corner of the red print in each 2" segment as shown. Stitch on the line. Trim away the corner, ¼" from the stitching. Finger-press the remaining triangle toward the corner to make Unit I.

Unit I
Make 4.

4. To make Unit II, position and stitch a yellow square to the upper left corner, and a green square to the upper right corner of each 2" x 3½" red rectangle. Trim ¼" from stitching. Turn the triangles toward the corners and press the yellow seam toward the red piece, and the green seam toward the outer corner.

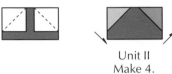

Unit II
Make 4.

5. Sew each Unit I to a Unit II. Press the seam toward Unit II.

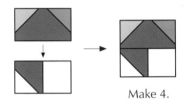

Make 4.

6. Arrange the units in 2 rows of 2 each with the yellow triangles forming the center of the block. Carefully pin each pair of units together where the triangles meet. Sew the units together and press the seams in the direction of the arrows. Sew the rows together; press the seam to one side.

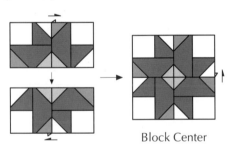

Block Center

7. To make the pieced-block border unit, position and stitch a 1½" green square to the upper right corner of each of the 2" x 3½" beige rectangles. Trim ¼" from the stitching and press the triangle toward the corner.

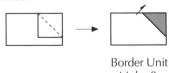

Border Unit
Make 8.

8. Sew the border units together in pairs as shown.

Border Strip
Make 4.

9. Pin a border strip to opposite sides of the poinsettia, matching seams carefully. Press the seams toward the poinsettia.

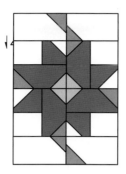

10. Sew a 2" red square to one end of each of the 2 remaining border units. Press the seam toward the red square. Sew a 2" green square to the other end. Press the seam toward the green square.

Make 2.

11. Sew the resulting strips to the remaining sides of the Poinsettia block. Note that the red and green squares alternate around the block at the outer corners. Press the seams toward the poinsettia.

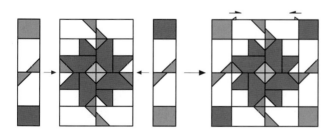

Assembling the Quilt Top

1. Arrange the blocks in 9 rows of 7 blocks each as shown in the quilt plan on page 25.
2. Sew the blocks together in horizontal rows, making sure to match the seams at the corners and leaves. Press the seams in opposite directions from row to row.

Press.

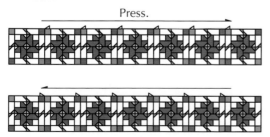

3. Join the rows, making sure to match the seams between the blocks, the corner squares, and the leaves.
4. Measure the quilt top for "Straight-Cut Borders" as shown on page 124. Cut 2½"-wide inner border strips from the green print and attach to the quilt top. Repeat for the outer borders, cutting strips 6" wide from the floral border fabric.

Finishing

Refer to pages 124–28 to finish your quilt.

1. Mark the quilt top with the desired quilting patterns or follow the quilting suggestion below.

2. Layer the quilt top with batting and backing; baste.
3. Quilt on the marked lines.
4. Add a hanging sleeve if desired.
5. Bind the edges with double-fold binding, using 2½"-wide straight-grain strips cut from the red-and-green print.
6. Sign your quilt. If this is a group quilt, have the participants sign the back of the quilt.

Starlight Angel

By Lora Rocke

Starlight Angel by Lora A. Rocke, 1995, Lincoln, Nebraska, 25" x 37".

LORA GREW UP ON THE PLAINS OF NEBRASKA AND ACQUIRED A LOVE OF ART AND NEEDLEWORK FROM HER GRANDMOTHER. SHE SAYS FONDLY, "GRAMMY TAUGHT ME A LITTLE BIT OF EVERYTHING. BUT MOSTLY SHE SHOWED ME HOW TO IMPROVISE WITH COLOR, DESIGN, AND MATERIALS."

IN 1972, LORA COMPLETED HER FIRST QUILT FROM PIECES HER GREAT-GRANDMOTHER STARTED. SINCE THEN, SHE HAS COMPLETED MORE THAN ONE HUNDRED THIRTY PROJECTS, A MAJORITY OF THEM ORIGINAL DESIGNS. LORA BEGAN PUBLISHING HER OWN PATTERNS IN 1992. SHE THINKS OF QUILTING AS A VERY DYNAMIC, CREATIVE ACTIVITY THAT ALLOWS HER TO PRODUCE A TRADITIONAL ART FORM QUICKLY. FOR LORA, CREATING SOMETHING PRACTICAL AND BEAUTIFUL AT THE SAME TIME IS THE "BEST OF BOTH WORLDS." LORA LIVES WITH HER HUSBAND AND DAUGHTER IN LINCOLN, NEBRASKA, WHERE SHE CREATES, TEACHES, WRITES, AND QUILTS.

LORA DESIGNED THIS YULETIDE ANGEL TO WELCOME FAMILY AND FRIENDS DURING THE HOLIDAYS. HER WATCHFUL POSE AND THE CASCADING STARS BENEATH HER WING REPRESENT BLESSINGS AND GOOD WISHES TO ALL. LORA USED QUICK-PIECING METHODS AND APPLIQUÉ TO CREATE THE ANGEL'S HEAVENLY SURROUNDINGS.

Quilt Size: 25" x 37"

Materials: 44"-wide fabric

1 yd. blue print for background, piecing, and binding

5/8 yd. total of assorted blue prints for stars and border

2" x 20" piece of purple solid for background and border

3/8 yd. total of assorted gold prints for pieced and appliquéd stars and halo

1/2 yd. white-on-white print for wing

1/4 yd. auburn print for angel's hair

6" x 12" piece of muslin for angel's face and shoulders

1 yd. for backing

29" x 41" piece of batting

Cutting

Using the pullout pattern, cut all appliqué shapes (face, hair, wing, shoulders, and stars) from the appropriate fabrics and prepare them, using your favorite appliqué method. (See pages 121–23). Cut the remaining pieces, listed below, using your rotary-cutting equipment.

From the blue print for the background, cut:
  1 piece, 9½" x 17"
  1 square, 18½" x 18½"
  1 square, 20" x 20", for the bias binding; use the remainder for the next cutting step

From the assorted blue prints and the blue print for the background, cut:
  175 squares, each 2" x 2", for the stars and the borders*
  2 pieces, each 2" x 5", for the background
  1 square, 3½" x 3½", for the background
  2 pieces, each 3½" x 5", for the background

From the purple solid, cut:
  10 squares, each 2" x 2", for the background

From the assorted gold prints, cut:
  9 squares, each 2" x 2", for the star centers
  22 squares, each 1¼" x 1¼", for the short star points
  38 squares, each 1¾" x 1¾", for the long star points
  21 pieces, each 2½" x 4½", for the foundation-pieced halo

Cut 2"-wide strips from each fabric, then crosscut 2" squares from the strips.

Making the Stars
Short Star Points

1. Draw a diagonal line from corner to corner on the wrong side of the 22 gold 1¼" squares. Place 1 square face down on the right side of each of 17 assorted blue 2" squares. Stitch on the line, chain piecing for efficiency.

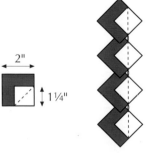

Chain-piece.

2. Trim the gold square only, ¼" from the stitching. Press the triangle toward the corner.

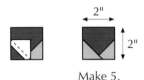

Press.

3. Set aside 12 of the resulting one-point squares. Add a gold square to the adjacent corner of the 5 remaining squares in the same manner.

Make 5.

Long Star Points

1. Draw a diagonal line from corner to corner on the wrong side of 38 gold 1¾" squares. Place 1 gold square face down on the right side of 1 blue 2" square. Repeat with the remaining squares. Stitch on the line, chain piecing for efficiency.
2. Trim the gold square only, ¼" from the stitching. Press the triangle toward the corner.
3. Repeat steps 1 and 2 on the adjacent corner of each blue square.

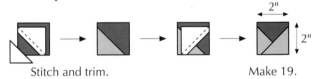

Stitch and trim.   Make 19.

Assembling the Background

1. Referring to the illustration below, arrange the completed star-point blocks, 8 of the gold 2" squares, and 37 of the small blue background pieces in 3 rows. Sew the pieces together as shown in each of the 3 rows.

Note: You will have 4 long star points left over for the star in the upper left corner of the quilt.

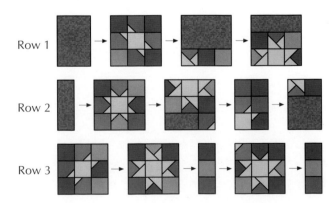

Row 1

Row 2

Row 3

2. Sew the rows together and press the seams in one direction. Sew the resulting piece to one long edge of the 9½" x 17" background piece. Press the seam toward the background.

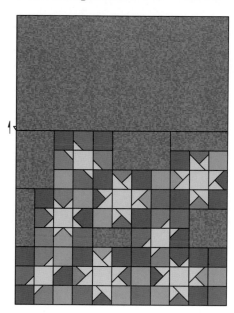

3. Make 4 Nine Patch blocks, using 34 assorted blue 2" squares and 2 purple 2" squares.

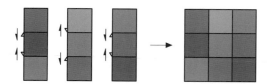

Make 4.

4. Join the 4 blocks in a row. Sew the resulting strip to one side of the 18½" background square. Press the seam toward the background.

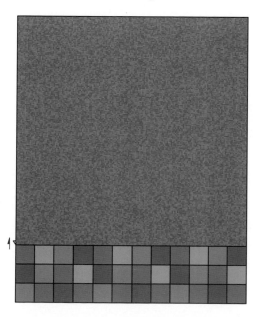

5. Join to the star section and press the seam toward the Nine Patch/background piece.

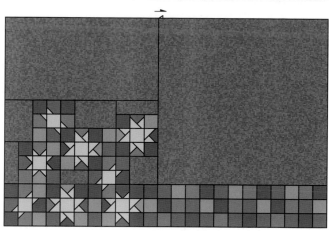

Making the Halo

To foundation-piece the halo, use the pattern on the pullout and 21 assorted gold 2½" x 4½" strips.

1. Trace the halo pattern onto a large piece of typing or tracing paper.
2. Arrange the assorted gold strips in the desired order, referring to the pullout pattern.
3. Place strip #1, right side up, on the unmarked side of the foundation pattern. Hold the foundation up to the light to check the placement, making sure the strip extends beyond all the lines. Pin strip in place.

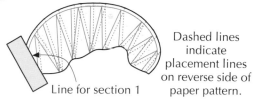

Line for section 1

Dashed lines indicate placement lines on reverse side of paper pattern.

4. Place fabric strip #2, face down, on strip #1. Pin.

Strip #2 face down on strip #1

5. Turn the foundation over and stitch on the line between strip #1 and #2, extending the stitching slightly past the ends of the line. Remove pins.

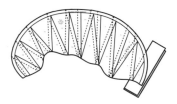

6. On the right side of the foundation, trim the excess fabric of both strips no less than ⅛" from the seam line. Flip strip #2 onto the foundation, finger-press the seam, and pin in place.

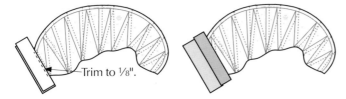

Trim to ⅛".

7. Add the remaining gold strips in the same manner to complete the halo. Carefully remove the paper foundation, tearing gently along the perforations on each seam line. Use needle-point tweezers to remove stray pieces of the foundation if necessary. Press the completed halo and trim the edges for appliqué.

Appliquéing the Angel

1. Before appliquéing the face to the background, trace the facial features onto the right side of the face fabric, using a permanent fabric marker.
2. Using your favorite method and referring to the quilt plan, appliqué the angel's face, hair, wing, and halo to the background in numerical order.

Assembling the Borders

Top Border

1. Using 42 assorted blue 2" squares and 2 purple 2" squares, make 22 two-patch units.

Make 22.

2. Sew a blue 2" square to 1 of the remaining long star-point squares.

Make 1.

3. Arrange the two-patch units in a row with the star-point square at the left end. Sew units together and press all seams in one direction.

Press.

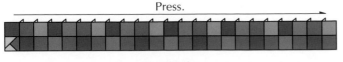

Top Border

4. Join the top border to the center section. Press the seam toward the center.

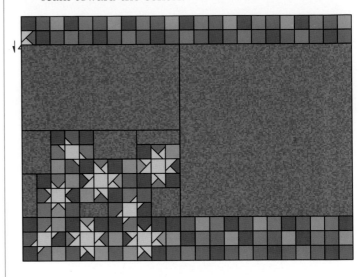

Side Border

1. Using 27 assorted blue 2" squares and the remaining purple 2" squares, make 14 two-patch units.

Make 14.

2. Sew a blue 2" square to each of 2 remaining long star-point squares, making sure to position the star points as shown.

Make 1.   Make 1.

3. Sew the remaining long star point to a gold 2" square.

Make 1.

4. Arrange the two-patch and star-point units as shown and sew together in a row. Press the seams in one direction.

Press.

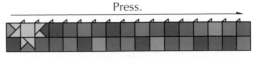

Side Border

5. Join the side border to the center section with the star points at the top. Press the seam toward the quilt top.

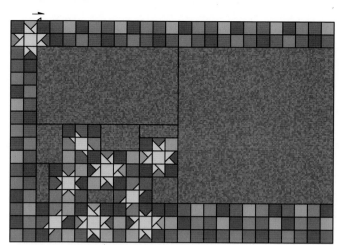

Finishing

Refer to pages 124–28 to finish your quilt.

1. Referring to the quilt plan on page 29, position and appliqué each star in place.
2. Layer the quilt top with batting and backing; baste.
3. Quilt as desired or try one or more of the following quilting suggestions as illustrated below:
   - Outline-quilt or echo-quilt around the Starlight Angel.
   - Quilt feathers on the wing.
   - Use metallic or shiny thread in the halo.
   - Machine doodle in the background.
   - Quilt spirals and circles on the stars and in the background.
4. Attach a hanging sleeve if desired.
5. Bind your quilt with double-fold binding, using 2½"-wide bias or straight-cut strips of the blue print.
6. Sign your quilt.

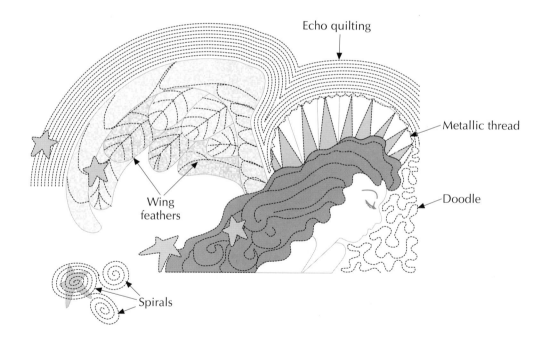

Echo quilting

Metallic thread

Doodle

Wing feathers

Spirals

Holiday Party!

By Lora Rocke

Holiday Party *by Lora A. Rocke, 1995, Lincoln, Nebraska, 36" x 48".*

WHEN LORA WAS DESIGNING THIS QUILTED WALL HANGING, SHE TRIED TO THINK OF ALL THE TRADITIONAL THINGS THAT WERE ALWAYS A PART OF HOLIDAY CELEBRATIONS IN HER FAMILY. STEAMING PUDDINGS AND COFFEE, LUSCIOUS PIES, COLORFUL RIBBONS AND CANDIES, AND THE GLOW OF CANDLES CAME TO MIND. LORA SAYS ASSEMBLING EACH MOTIF IN A STRIP REMINDED HER OF HOLIDAY TABLES SET WITH ROWS AND ROWS OF CHRISTMAS GOODIES.

HANG THIS COLORFUL WALL HANGING, AND YOUR FAMILY WILL BE CLAMORING FOR PLUM PUDDINGS, PIES, AND PRESENTS. MADE WITH QUICK MACHINE-PIECING AND APPLIQUÉ TECHNIQUES, THIS DELIGHTFUL QUILT WILL TAKE NO TIME AT ALL TO CREATE.

Quilt Size: 36" x 48"

Materials: 44"-wide fabric

2³⁄₄ yds. white print for background and borders

¹⁄₄ yd. green print #1 for leaves, candy, and tablecloth

¹⁄₄ yd. red print for tablecloth, cups, saucers, and candy

¹⁄₄ yd. black print for tablecloth and candy

¹⁄₄ yd. stripe for candlesticks and candy

¹⁄₄ yd. medium yellow print for candle flames and candy

¹⁄₄ yd. dark yellow print for flames

¹⁄₄ yd. green print #2 for plates, cups, and saucers

¹⁄₄ yd. plum print for puddings

¹⁄₄ yd. cream print for icings

¹⁄₄ yd. brown print for piecrusts

¹⁄₈ yd. each of 4 fruit-colored prints for pies

1¹⁄₈ yds. multicolored print for cups, bows, ribbon border, and binding

¹⁄₄ yd. dark blue print for ribbon border

1¹⁄₂ yds. for backing

40" x 52" piece of batting

3 to 6 red buttons, each ³⁄₈" in diameter

3. Sew a background triangle A to each side of 3 star blocks. Press seams toward the triangles. Each block should measure 5" x 5".

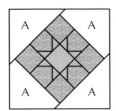

Make 3.

4. Sew a corner triangle A to 2 corners of the remaining star blocks. Sew a corner triangle B to the other 2 corners of each block. Press the seams toward the triangles. Reserve these 2 blocks for the ends of the flame row. Trim to measure 5" x 5¾".

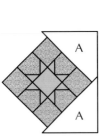

Make 2.

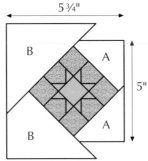

Make 2.

5. Arrange the star-flame blocks in a row, placing a 5" x 5¾" block at each end. Sew the blocks together and press the seams in one direction. The finished row should measure 5" x 24½".

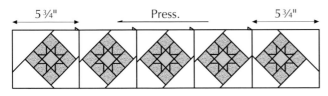

Star-Flame Row

Plum Pudding

1. Draw a diagonal line from corner to corner on the wrong side of 6 background 2" squares. Position and stitch a square to 2 corners of each green 2" x 8½" plate piece. Trim the square only and press.

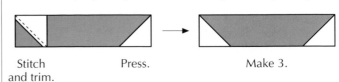

Stitch and trim.   Press.   Make 3.

2. Using your favorite appliqué method (pages 121–23) and aligning the bottom edges, appliqué a plum pudding to the center of each 5" x 8½" background piece.

Make 3.

3. Join each plate section to the bottom edge of a plum pudding section. Press the seam toward the plate.

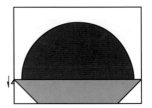

4. Appliqué icing and holly leaves to each pudding.

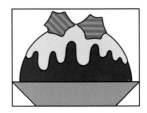

5. Arrange the plum pudding blocks in a row and join. Press the seams in one direction. The finished row should measure 6½" x 24½".

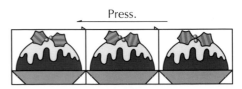

Plum Pudding Row

Pies

For each pie, use four 3" squares—1 of background fabric, 1 of crust fabric, and 2 of pie fabric. Each piece of pie requires 4 half-square triangle units made from these squares. You will need a 6" Bias Square ruler.

Make 4 units per pie.

1. For each piece of pie, place a 3" background square face down on a pie-print square. Draw a diagonal line on the wrong side of the background square. Stitch 1/4" from the line on both sides of the line; press. Cut on the diagonal line. Open each section and press toward the darker fabric. Place the diagonal line of the Bias Square ruler on the seam line of each unit and trim to 2 1/2" x 2 1/2". Repeat with 1 square of pie fabric and 1 square of crust fabric for each piece of pie.

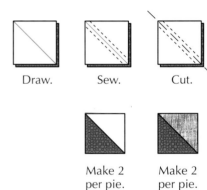

Draw.   Sew.   Cut.   Press.

Make 2 per pie.   Make 2 per pie.

2. Arrange the half-square triangle units for each piece of pie in 2 rows. Sew the units together in rows, pressing the seams in opposite directions. Sew the rows together and press the seam toward the point.

Make 4.

3. Sew a 1 1/2" x 4 1/2" background piece to each 1 1/2" x 4 1/2" crust piece. Press the seam toward the crust. Sew 1 of the resulting units to the top edge of each piece of pie. Press the seam toward the crust.

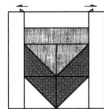

Make 4.

4. Sew a 1 1/2" x 6 1/2" background piece to each side of each piece of pie. Press the seams toward the background pieces.

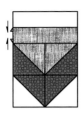

Make 4.

5. Sew the 4 pie blocks together in a row and press the seams in one direction. The row should measure 6 1/2" x 24 1/2".

Cups

1. Draw a diagonal line from corner to corner on the wrong side of eight 2" background squares. Position and stitch a square to 2 corners of each 2" x 6 1/2" green and each 2" x 6 1/2" red saucer piece. Trim the square only and press.

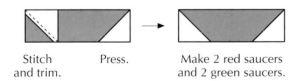

Stitch and trim.   Press.   Make 2 red saucers and 2 green saucers.

2. Arrange the pieces for each cup and sew together as shown. Press the seams in the direction of the arrows.

Make 4.

4. Arrange the border pieces in alternating fashion as shown and sew together to make 2 side border strips. Press seams in the direction of the arrows.

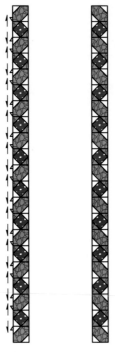

Left Side   Right Side

5. Join a ribbon border to each long side of the quilt top. Press the seams toward the background strips.

Finishing

Refer to pages 124–28 to finish your quilt.

1. Attach the outer border strips, following the directions for "Borders with Mitered Corners," page 125.
2. Trim and square the edges of the quilt top to measure 36" x 48".
3. Layer the quilt top with batting and backing; baste.
4. Quilt as desired or try one or more of the following:
   - Quilt fire in the flames.
   - Use a specialty thread to create decorations on the plum puddings.
   - Quilt steam rising from the cups.
   - Quilt a zigzag line along the top edge of the piecrusts for "crimping."
   - Quilt a repeat of the ribbon border shape in the outer borders.

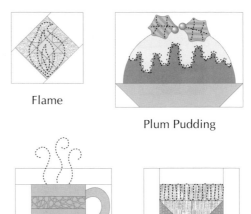

Flame   Plum Pudding

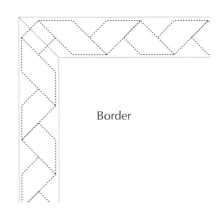

Steam   Crimped Pie Crust

Border

5. Sew 1 or 2 small red buttons beside the holly leaves on the plum puddings for berries.
6. Add a hanging sleeve if desired.
7. Bind the quilt with double-fold binding, using 2½"-wide bias or straight-grain strips cut from the multicolored print.
8. Sign your quilt.

Appliqué and Quilting Templates

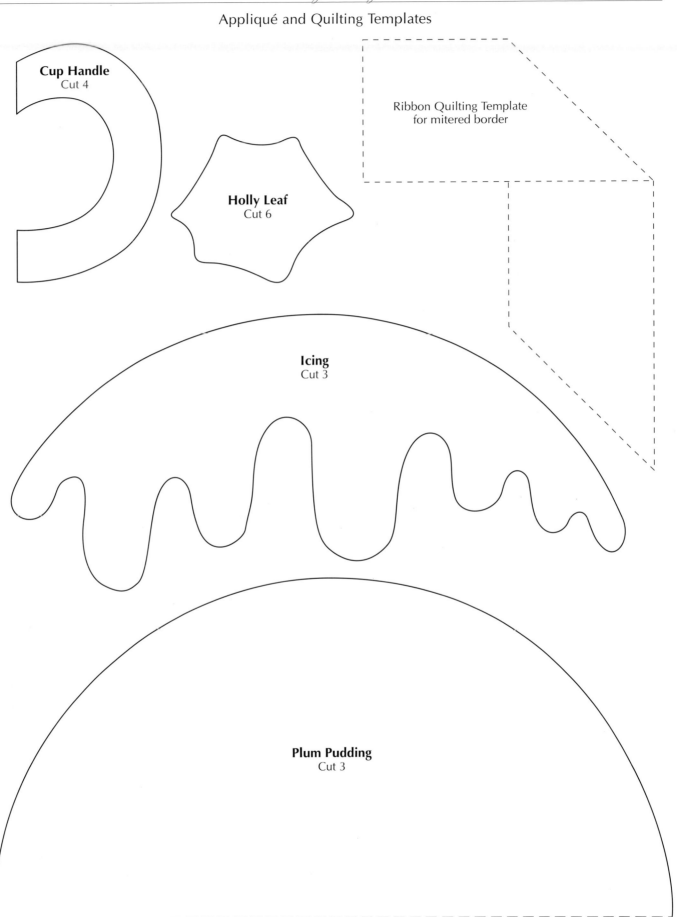

Cup Handle
Cut 4

Holly Leaf
Cut 6

Ribbon Quilting Template
for mitered border

Icing
Cut 3

Plum Pudding
Cut 3

Jolly Old Soul

By Michele O'Neil Kincaid

Jolly Old Soul *by Michele O'Neil Kincaid, 1995, Strafford, New Hampshire, 48¹/₂″ x 48¹/₂″.*

MICHELE O'NEIL KINCAID

MICHELE BEGAN QUILTMAKING IN 1977 TO MAKE A QUILT FOR HER WEDDING. SHE REFERS TO THAT FIRST ATTEMPT AS A "HEAVENLY DISASTER." HOWEVER, THAT FIRST QUILT LED TO OTHERS, AND NOW MICHELE CAN'T SEEM TO FIND TIME TO COOK AND CLEAN BECAUSE SHE IS BUSY DESIGNING QUILTS FOR *CREATIVE QUILTING*, *QUICK AND EASY QUILTMAKING*, AND *QUILT WORLD* MAGAZINES. SHE ALSO PUBLISHES HER OWN LINE OF PATTERNS.

WITH A BACKGROUND IN CRAFTS AND DRESSMAKING, MICHELE FOUND IT ONLY NATURAL TO COMBINE QUILTMAKING WITH GARMENT SEWING. ONE OF HER GARMENTS WAS FEATURED IN THE 1993–94 FAIRFIELD FASHION SHOW. SHE ALSO CREATES ONE-OF-A-KIND WEDDING DRESSES AND FIBER ART.

AN ACTIVE MEMBER OF THE COCHECO QUILT GUILD, MICHELE LIVES IN NEW HAMPSHIRE WITH HER HUSBAND AND TWO DAUGHTERS. OTHER FAVORITE PASTIMES INCLUDE GARDENING, COOKING, COLLECTING ANTIQUES, AND SPENDING TIME WITH FRIENDS.

"JOLLY OLD SOUL" CAME TO LIFE ON MICHELE'S COMPUTER SCREEN. THE STARS DEVELOPED FROM DOODLES. THE SANTA APPLIQUÉ CAME LATER, WHEN THE CENTER OF THE PIECED DESIGN SCREAMED FOR SOMETHING. THE PIECING IS EASY, REQUIRING ONLY SQUARES, RECTANGLES, AND THREE DIFFERENT TRIANGLE SHAPES. NEEDLE-TURN APPLIQUÉ AND A FEW BRUSH STROKES FINISH OFF MICHELE'S "JOLLY OLD SOUL," DRESSED IN REGAL FABRICS.

Block A
Make 16 red/dark beige.
Make 12 gold/dark beige.
Make 4 gold/light beige.

Block B
Make 16 red/dark beige.
Make 12 gold/dark beige.
Make 4 gold/light beige.

Block C
Make 16.

Quilt Size: 48½" x 48½"

Materials: 44"-wide fabric

2 yds. dark beige print for background

½ yd. light beige print for Santa background

⅔ yd. dark green print for star centers and triangles

½ yd. red print for star points

½ yd. gold print for star points

1 fat quarter (18" x 22") "regal" print for coat

1 fat quarter (18" x 22") medium blue print for lining

1 fat quarter (18" x 22") gold print for garment

Scrap of rust print for pants and mittens

Scrap of gray print for beard

Scrap of red print for apples in sack

Scrap of gray print for sack

Scrap of flesh tone for face

Scrap of black for boots and belt

Scrap of beige or off-white for fur

Scrap of polyester fiberfill

Fabric paint or markers for details

3 yds. fabric for backing

52" x 52" piece of batting

Cutting

*Use the piecing templates on page 49 and
the appliqué pattern on the pullout.*
Cut all strips across the fabric width (crosswise
grain). Save all fabric leftovers for the pieced binding.

From the dark beige print, cut:
  10 strips, each 4¹/₂" x 42"; crosscut into 80
    squares, each 4¹/₂" x 4¹/₂", and 4 rectangles,
    each 4¹/₂" x 8¹/₂"
  4 strips, each 2¹/₂" x 42"; crosscut into 64
    squares, each 2¹/₂" x 2¹/₂"
  4 of Template A and 4 of Template A reversed
  8 of Template C

From the light beige print, cut:
  3 strips, each 4¹/₂" x 42"; crosscut into 16
    squares, each 4¹/₂" x 4¹/₂", and 4 rectangles,
    each 4¹/₂" x 8¹/₂"

From the dark green print, cut:
  2 strips, each 4¹/₂" x 42"; crosscut into 16
    squares, each 4¹/₂" x 4¹/₂", for Block C
  4 of Template B and 4 of Template B reversed

From the red print for star points, cut:
  6 strips, each 2¹/₂" x 42"; crosscut into 32
    squares, each 2¹/₂" x 2¹/₂", and 32 rectangles,
    each 2¹/₂" x 4¹/₂"

From the gold print for star points, cut:
  6 strips, each 2¹/₂" x 42"; crosscut 2 of the strips
    into 32 squares, each 2¹/₂" x 2¹/₂". From the
    remaining strips, cut 32 rectangles, each
    2¹/₂" x 4¹/₂".

Piecing

1. Draw a diagonal line from
   corner to corner on the wrong
   side of each 2¹/₂" dark beige,
   gold, and red square.

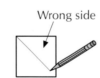

Wrong side

Make: 64 dark beige
32 gold
32 red

2. On the wrong side of 16 of the red 2¹/₂" x 4¹/₂"
   rectangles and 16 of the gold 2¹/₂" x 4¹/₂" rectangles,
   draw a diagonal line from corner to corner. Repeat
   with the remaining rectangles, reversing the direction of the line as shown.

Wrong side

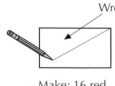

Make: 16 red   Make: 16 red
16 gold   16 gold

3. To make Block A, position a 2¹/₂" red square face
   down on the right side of a 4¹/₂" dark beige square
   in the lower right corner. Stitch on the line and
   trim ¹/₄" from the stitching. Repeat with 15 more
   red squares and 12 gold squares. Press the seam
   toward the triangle in each unit. Repeat with 4
   gold 2¹/₂" squares and 4 light beige 4¹/₂" squares.

Make 16.   Make 16.   Make 4.

4. Position a red rectangle, right side down, on the
   right side of each red/dark beige square in the lower
   left corner. Stitch on the line and trim ¹/₄" from
   the stitching. Repeat with gold rectangles and the
   gold/dark beige squares, and with gold rectangles
   and the light beige/gold squares. Press the seam
   toward the triangle in each block.

Block A   Block A   Block A
Make 16.   Make 12.   Make 4.

Note: When joined, the star points will be ¹/₄" from
the block corners, so the stars appear to float on
the background.

5. To make Block B, repeat steps 3 and 4, *reversing
   the position of the squares and rectangles*.

Block B   Block B   Block B
Make 16.   Make 12.   Make 4.

6. To make Block C, sew a dark beige 2¹/₂" square to
   opposite corners of each 4¹/₂" dark green square.
   Cut ¹/₄" from the stitching and press the seams
   toward the triangles. Repeat on the remaining 2
   corners of each square.

Block C
Make 16.

7. Assemble Blocks D and E as shown below, using the triangles cut with Templates A, B, and C.

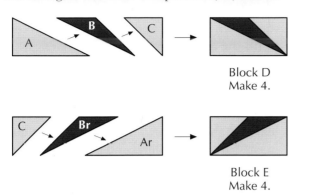

Block D
Make 4.

Block E
Make 4.

8. Referring to the illustrations, assemble Sections 1, 2, 3, and the center panel.

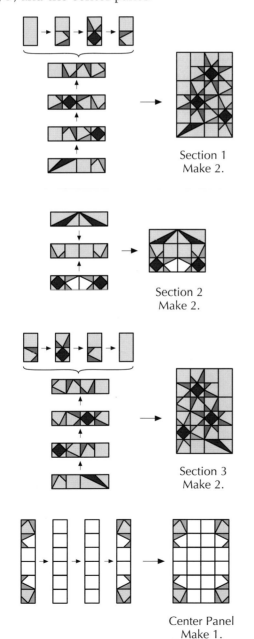

Section 1
Make 2.

Section 2
Make 2.

Section 3
Make 2.

Center Panel
Make 1.

9. Sew each Section 1 to a Section 3. Set the pieced units aside.

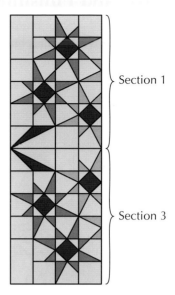

⎱ Section 1

⎱ Section 3

Appliquéing the Santa

Refer to "Needle-Turn Appliqué" on page 123.

1. Make 2 full-size photocopies or tracings of the Santa pattern on the pullout. Set 1 aside to use as a guide. Trace pieces 14–17, 24–26, 28–29, and the apples in the sack onto a separate sheet of tracing paper. Number the pieces and cut out. Cut the remaining full-size copy apart into pieces for paper templates.

2. Place each paper template *face up on the right side* of the appropriate fabric and trace around the edge. Trace the facial features onto the face piece and the quilting lines onto the beard piece. Cut out each piece 1/4" beyond the traced line.

3. Working on a light box or at a large window, place the pieced center panel on top of the photocopy you set aside. Lightly trace the Santa outline onto the center panel.

4. Referring to the pattern, appliqué the pieces in numerical order, using needle-turn appliqué or another favorite method. Tuck a bit of polyester fiberfill under the beard and sack appliqués. Sew the mustache in place.

5. Paint or embroider branches and holly on the hood.

6. Paint or use fabric markers for lips, eyes, cheeks, and eyebrows. Paint on belt buckle and boot ties.

Angels of Bethlehem

by Virda Wilcox Lawrence

Angels of Bethlehem by *Virda Wilcox Lawrence*, 1994, Lakebay, Washington, 88³/4″ x 88³/4″ (not including Prairie Points).

VIRDA WILCOX LAWRENCE

VIRDA OWES HER LOVE OF HANDWORK TO HER MOTHER AND GRANDMOTHER, WHO TAUGHT HER TO EMBROIDER, CROCHET, AND SEW. AT THE AGE OF EIGHTEEN, SHE LEARNED TO QUILT AT A CHURCH WOMEN'S AUXILIARY MEETING. SHE SAYS SHE WISHES SOMEONE HAD TOLD HER HIGH SCHOOL GEOMETRY WOULD APPLY TO QUILTING; SHE WOULD HAVE PAID MORE ATTENTION!

VIRDA HAS BEEN ACTIVE IN THE QUILTING WORLD EVER SINCE. SHE LOVES TO CONTINUALLY INCREASE HER KNOWLEDGE BY ATTENDING AND TEACHING WORKSHOPS. SHE CALLS THE CLASSROOM A "JOINT VENTURE" BECAUSE HER STUDENTS LEARN FROM HER, AND SHE ALSO LEARNS FROM THEM.

VIRDA LOVES PEOPLE AND SHE LOVES TO QUILT. BESIDES TEACHING FOR SEVERAL LOCAL QUILT SHOPS IN WASHINGTON STATE, VIRDA HAS ALSO TAUGHT IN JAPAN AND ALASKA. SHE IS PAST PRESIDENT AND NEWSLETTER EDITOR OF THE PORT ORCHARD QUILTERS' GUILD, PAST CHAPTER COORDINATOR FOR THE NATIONAL QUILTING ASSOCIATION, CLOTHING AND TEXTILE ADVISOR FOR PIERCE COUNTY, AND HAS TAUGHT 4-H SUMMER SEWING CLASSES.

ABOUT "ANGELS OF BETHLEHEM," VIRDA WRITES: "I WAS BORN ON CHRISTMAS EVE AND I HAD ALWAYS WANTED A SPECIAL CHRISTMAS QUILT. AFTER THINKING ABOUT IT OFF AND ON FOR SEVERAL YEARS, I FINALLY DECIDED I WANTED A QUILT THAT REPRESENTED THE REAL REASON WE CELEBRATE CHRISTMAS. I THOUGHT ABOUT THE HUMBLE CIRCUMSTANCES OF THE SAVIOR'S BIRTH—THE BRIGHT STAR AND HERALDING ANGELS WITH THEIR JOYOUS MESSAGE FOR THE WORLD. MY LOVE FOR MUSIC AND MY EXPERIENCE AS A FLORAL DESIGNER FOUND THEIR WAY INTO THE DESIGN AS WELL. THE OTHER SOURCE OF INSPIRATION WAS MY DEAR SISTER, JUDIE RENEE SMITH, WHO IS IN CONSTANT PAIN, BUT CONTINUES TO FIGHT THE GOOD FIGHT WITH HER SMILE AND CHEERFUL ATTITUDE. SHE IS A GREAT EXAMPLE TO ME, FOR YOU SEE, SHE IS A REAL ANGEL."

Quilt Size: 88³/₄" x 88³/₄"
(not including Prairie Points)

Materials: 44"-wide fabric

Note: When choosing fabrics for the star, refer to the color photo and to the illustration at the top of the next page to identify each of the required colors.

¼ yd. green print #1 (Color 1)

³/₈ yd. red print #1 (Color 2)

½ yd. red/tan print (Color 3)

¾ yd. green print #2 (Color 4)

1 yd. red print or solid #2 (Color 5)

½ yd. cream/red/green print (Color 6)

Starry Geese

By Johanna Wilson

Starry Geese by Johanna Wilson, 1994, Walnut Grove, Minnesota, 32" x 32".

JOHANNA WILSON

JOHANNA IS THE OWNER OF PLUM CREEK PATCHWORK IN WALNUT GROVE, MINNESOTA. SHE HAS BEEN QUILTING SINCE A FRIEND GAVE HER AN ANTIQUE QUILT TOP TO COMPLETE. AS A RESULT OF HER HOW-TO-FINISH-THE-TOP RESEARCH, JOHANNA BEGAN DESIGNING QUILTS AND PATTERNS AND HAS SINCE PUBLISHED MORE THAN TWENTY-FIVE QUILT PATTERNS AND A BOOK BASED ON THE QUILTS IN THE *LITTLE HOUSE* BOOKS BY LAURA INGALLS WILDER.

JOHANNA WAS A TEACHER AND HIGH SCHOOL LIBRARIAN IN CONNECTICUT BEFORE MOVING WITH HER HUSBAND, ORMON, TO A FARM ON THE MINNESOTA PRAIRIE. IN THE PAST SEVEN YEARS, SHE HAS EXHIBITED HER QUILTS IN SHOWS, MUSEUMS, AND EXHIBITIONS ACROSS THE UNITED STATES AND EUROPE, WINNING VARIOUS AWARDS FOR HER DESIGNS. SHE WAS THE RECIPIENT OF THE FIRST MASTER/APPRENTICESHIP FOLK ARTS TEACHING GRANT IN QUILTING FROM THE MINNESOTA ARTS BOARD IN 1990. SHE ENJOYS TEACHING TO SHARE THE JOY AND PROMOTE THE ART OF QUILTING.

IN THE 1980S, JOHANNA BEGAN TEACHING QUILT CLASSES AND WANTED HER BEGINNING QUILTERS TO UNDERSTAND AND APPRECIATE THE IMPACT OF COLOR AND TEXTURE FOR ARTISTIC EXPRESSION. A NATURAL OUTCOME OF HER PHILOSOPHY OF TEACHING AND ADVENTURESOME SPIRIT WAS AN ORIGINAL QUILT PATTERN FOR EACH CLASS. "STARRY GEESE" WAS THE FIRST OF MANY SUCH PATTERNS.

THE CHRISTMAS VERSION OF "STARRY GEESE" FEATURES AN ASSORTMENT OF RED AND GREEN SCRAPS ON A WARM TAN "SNOWFLAKE" BACKGROUND. JOHANNA AUDITIONED EACH OF HER SCRAPS FOR A PLACE IN THE QUILT. AN OLD FAVORITE FOUND A SPECIAL PLACE IN THE CORNER SQUARES, BUT BECAUSE THERE WASN'T QUITE ENOUGH, SOME OF THE STAR POINTS DO NOT MATCH. CAN YOU FIND THEM? STIPPLED MACHINE QUILTING ADDS TEXTURE TO THE BACKGROUND, AND HAND QUILTING ENHANCES THE STAR CENTERS.

Quilt Size: 32" x 32"

Materials: 44"-wide fabric

1 1/4 yds. light tan for background

1/3 yd. total of 1 or more dark green prints for stars

1/4 yd. total of assorted red checks, plaids, and stripes for flying geese

1/4 yd. total of assorted green checks, plaids, and stripes for flying geese

1 yd. for backing

36" x 36" piece of batting

1/2 yd. red stripe for binding

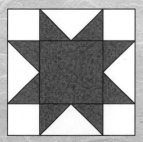

Star Block

61

Cutting and Piecing
Center Star

1. **From the light tan background fabric, cut:**
   1 strip, 3⅜" x 12"; crosscut into 4 squares, each 3⅜" x 3⅜"
   1 square, 4⅜" x 4⅜"; cut twice diagonally to yield 4 quarter-square triangles

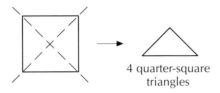

4 quarter-square triangles

2. **From the dark green print, cut:**
   1 square, 4½" x 4½", for the center
   1 strip, 2⅞"x 24"; crosscut into 4 squares, each 2⅞" x 2⅞"; cut once diagonally to yield 8 half-square triangles for the star points

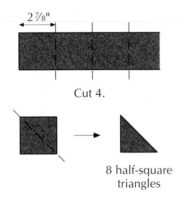

2⅞"

Cut 4.

8 half-square triangles

3. **From the red plaid fabric, cut:**
   2 squares, each 6⅞" x 6⅞"; cut once diagonally to yield 4 half-square triangles

4. Sew 1 green triangle to 2 adjacent sides of each 3⅜" background square. Press the seams toward the green triangles.

5. Sew 2 of the resulting units to opposite sides of the 4½" green square. Press the seams away from the square.

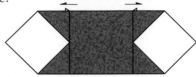

6. Sew 1 of the remaining background triangles to each end of the 2 remaining units. Press the seams toward the green triangles.

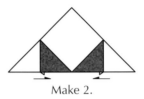

Make 2.

7. Sew the resulting triangles to opposite sides of the center square to complete the center star. This star should measure 9" x 9", including seam allowances.

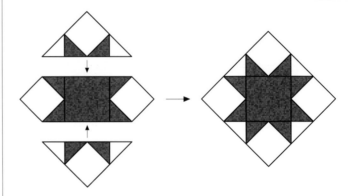

8. Sew a red triangle to opposite sides of the center star. The block should now measure 12½"x 12½", including seam allowances.

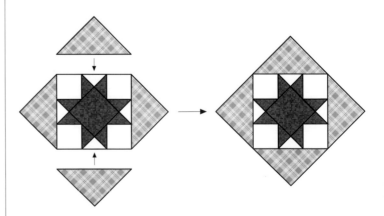

Center Star Border

1. **From the assorted green fabrics, cut:**
   12 squares, each 2⅞" x 2⅞"; cut once diagonally to yield 24 triangles
2. **From the light tan background fabric, cut:**
   1 strip, 2½" x 12"; crosscut into 4 squares, each 2½" x 2½"
   1 strip, 2⅞" x 38"; crosscut into 12 squares, each 2⅞" x 2⅞"; cut once diagonally to yield 24 triangles
3. Sew the triangles together in pairs to make 24 half-square triangle units. Press the seam toward the green triangle in each unit.

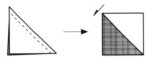

Make 24.

4. Arrange the units as shown to make 4 identical rows. Sew the units together in each row and press the seams toward the green triangles. *Press the center seam open.*

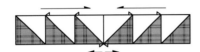

Press center seam open.
Make 4.

5. Sew a row to the top and bottom edges of the center star. Press the seams toward the star.

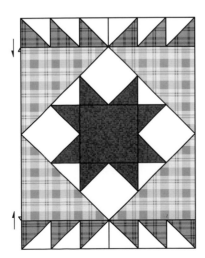

6. Sew one 2½" background square to each end of the remaining rows of half-square triangle units. Press the seams toward the green triangles.

Make 2.

7. Sew the resulting rows to the sides of the center square. Press the seams toward the center.

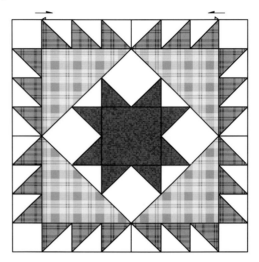

Flying Geese Strips

1. **From the assorted red and green fabrics, cut:**
   32 rectangles, each 2½" x 4½", for the geese
2. **From the light tan background fabric, cut:**
   8 strips, each 2½" x 42"; crosscut into 8 strips, each 2½" x 16½", for the inner and outer sashing strips, and 64 squares, each 2½" x 2½", for the geese
3. Draw a diagonal line from corner to corner on the wrong side of each 2½" background square. Place a square face down on one end of a rectangle and stitch on the marked line. Trim only the square ¼" from the stitching. Press the triangle toward the corner of the rectangle. Repeat with another 2½" background square at the opposite end of the rectangle.

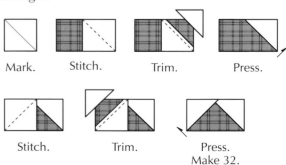

Mark.　Stitch.　Trim.　Press.

Stitch.　Trim.　Press.
Make 32.

Potholder Tips

- Choose medium- to dark-value prints to hide food stains.
- Insert an 8½" square of prewashed, cotton pinwale corduroy between the pieced block and the polyester fleece for a flatter potholder.
- If you wish, substitute three layers of prewashed, cotton pinwale corduroy for the polyester fleece. After washing, the finished potholder will need to be smoothed out.
- To make multiples of potholders #1 and #2, use strip-piecing methods.
- When doing paper foundation piecing, as shown for the Starburst potholder, use a short stitch length to make paper removal easier.
- Bias-cut binding wears better than straight-cut binding. See the special binding method on page 71.

Potholder #1: Chinese Coin

Materials

10 rectangles, each 2" x 4", cut from assorted red prints

2 squares, each 8½" x 8½", of Thermolam® or similar thin polyester fleece

8½" x 8½" square of fabric for backing

2⅝" x 36" bias strip of black-with-gold print for binding

Piecing

1. Sew rectangles together in 2 rows of 5 each. Press the seams in opposite directions from row to row. Sew the rows together to complete the block. Trim to 7½" square.

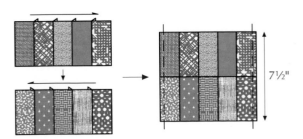

2. Layer the pieced square with the 2 squares of fleece and the backing. Using straight pins, pin through all layers at the corners and in the center.
3. Machine quilt through all layers ¼" from the horizontal and vertical seams.

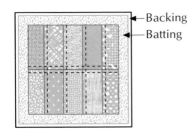

4. Trim the fleece and backing even with the outer edges of the pieced square.
5. Bind the potholder, following the directions in the sidebar on page 71.

Potholder #2: Framed Pinwheel

Materials

4" x 4" square of red print #1 for corner squares

3" x 3" square of red print #1 for pinwheel

2 squares, each 2⅝" x 2⅝", of green solid fabric for pinwheel

4¾" x 4¾" square of green-on-white print for outer triangles

6" x 6" square of white-on-black print for block frame

2 squares, each 8½" x 8½", of Thermolam or similar thin polyester fleece

8½" x 8½" square of fabric for backing

2⅝" x 36" bias strip of white-on-black print for binding

Cutting and Piecing

1. Cut 2 squares of green pinwheel fabric and 2 squares of red print #2, each 2⅝" x 2⅝". Cut each square once diagonally for 8 half-square triangles.

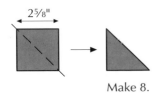

Make 8.

2. Sew each red print #2 triangle to a green triangle and press the seam toward the red triangle.

Make 4.

3. Arrange the squares in 2 rows of 2 each as shown. Sew the blocks together in rows and press the seams in opposite directions. Sew the rows together.

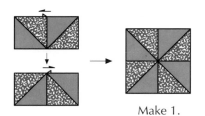

Make 1.

4. Cut the 4³/4" square of green-on-white print twice diagonally to create 4 quarter-square triangles.

5. Sew 1 green-on-white triangle to each side of the pinwheel.

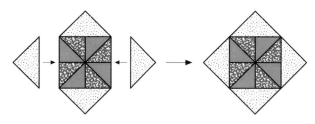

6. Cut 4 rectangles of white-on-black fabric, each 1¹/2" x 5³/8". Cut 4 squares of red print #1, each 1¹/2" x 1¹/2". Sew 1 red #1 square to each end of 2 of the white-on-black rectangles. Press the seams toward the rectangles.

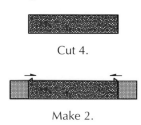

Cut 4.

Make 2.

7. Sew a white-on-black rectangle to opposite sides of the pinwheel unit. Press the seams toward the rectangles. Sew the units made in step 6 to the pinwheel unit. Press.

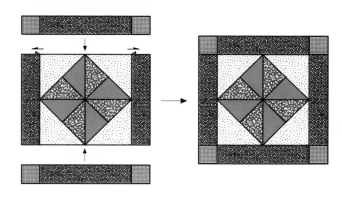

8. Layer the pieced square with the 2 squares of fleece and the backing. Using straight pins, pin through all layers at the corners and in the center.
9. Machine quilt in-the-ditch around the outer edges of the pinwheel and along the edges of the green-on-white triangles.

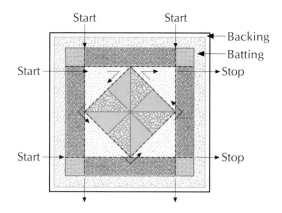

10. Trim the fleece and backing even with the outer edges of the pieced square.
11. Bind the potholder, following the directions in the sidebar on page 71.

Potholder #3: Boxes and Bars

Materials

Scraps of reds (or other colors of your choice) for boxes

$1\frac{3}{4}$" x $7\frac{1}{2}$" strip of white-on-black print for 1 bar

1" x $7\frac{1}{2}$" strip of black-on-white print for 1 bar

2 squares, each $8\frac{1}{2}$" x $8\frac{1}{2}$", of Thermolam or similar thin polyester fleece

$8\frac{1}{2}$" x $8\frac{1}{2}$" square of fabric for backing

$2\frac{5}{8}$" x 36" x 36" bias strip of black-on-white print for binding

Cutting and Piecing

1. From scraps, cut 12 squares, each $2\frac{1}{4}$" x $2\frac{1}{4}$". Sew the squares together in 3 rows of 4 squares each. Press seams in opposite directions from row to row. Sew the rows together to create a twelve-patch unit.

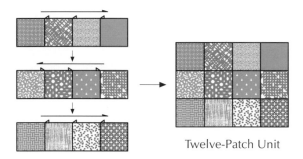

Twelve-Patch Unit

2. Sew the white-on-black strip to the black-on-white strip. Press the seam toward the darker strip.

3. Sew the resulting unit to one long edge of the twelve-patch unit.

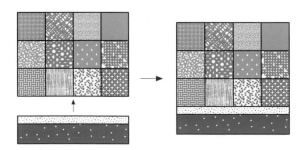

4. Layer the pieced square with the 2 squares of fleece and the backing. Using straight pins, pin through all layers at the corners and in the center.

5. Machine outline-quilt $\frac{1}{4}$" from one side of each seam.

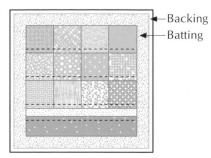

Backing
Batting

6. Trim the fleece and backing even with the outer edges of the pieced square.

7. Bind the potholder, following the directions in the sidebar on page 71.

Potholder #4: Starburst

Materials

6 strips, each $2\frac{1}{4}$" x 7", of white-on-black print for rays

2 strips, each $2\frac{1}{4}$" x 7", of light green solid for rays

2 strips, each $2\frac{1}{4}$" x 7", of medium green solid for rays

$2\frac{3}{4}$" x 8" strip of dark green solid for rays

$4\frac{7}{8}$" x $4\frac{7}{8}$" square of medium green solid for corner

$8\frac{1}{2}$" x $8\frac{1}{2}$" square of fabric for backing

2 squares, each $8\frac{1}{2}$" x $8\frac{1}{2}$", of Thermolam or similar thin polyester fleece

$2\frac{5}{8}$" x 36" bias strip of white-on-black print for binding

1 sheet computer, tracing, or typing paper

Foundation Piecing

1. Trace the complete starburst pattern on page 72 onto computer, tracing, or typing paper. Cut out at least $\frac{1}{4}$" outside the outer line of the traced design.

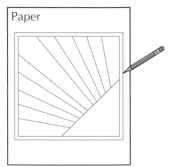

Paper

Trace pattern.

2. Working on the wrong side of the paper pattern, position a strip of the white-on-black print right side up over the first ray. Hold the paper up to the light to make sure the fabric strip extends at least ¼" beyond each of the ray lines. Pin in place.

3. Pin a strip of light green on top of the first strip with right sides together and raw edges even.

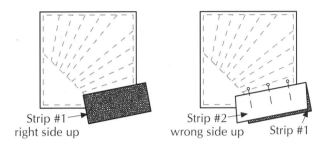

Strip #1
right side up

Strip #2
wrong side up   Strip #1

Dashed lines indicate stitching lines
on the reverse side of paper pattern.

4. Turn the paper over and stitch on the line between the first 2 rays. Remove the pins and trim the seam allowance to ¼", then flip the light green ray over and finger-press in place. Trim even with the outer edges of the foundation only.

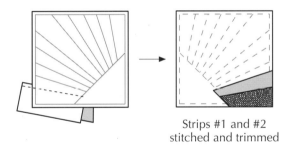

Strips #1 and #2
stitched and trimmed

Note: It may be necessary to grade the seam allowances to prevent dark fabrics from shadowing through lighter fabrics.

5. Continue adding pieces in the same manner, sewing, flipping, finger pressing, and pressing until all rays have been sewn in place. Refer to the diagram and photo for color placement.

6. Add the medium green corner triangle in the same manner.

7. Press the completed block and trim to 7½" square. Remove the paper, tearing away carefully along each stitching line.

8. Layer the pieced square with the 2 squares of fleece and the backing. Using straight pins, pin through all layers at the corners and in the center.

9. Stitch in-the-ditch along the ray seam lines and ¼" from the seam line in the corner triangle.

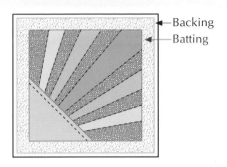

←Backing
←Batting

10. Trim the fleece and backing even with the outer edges of the pieced square.

11. Bind the potholder, following the directions in the sidebar below.

Reverse Binding for Potholders

Use this method to apply binding by machine; no hand stitching is necessary. You will need a strip of bias binding, 2⅝" x 36", for each potholder.

1. Fold the binding strip in half, wrong sides together, and press.

2. Pin and sew the binding *to the backing side of the potholder*, mitering the corners as shown for double-fold binding on pages 127–28.

3. Turn the binding over the raw edges to the right side of the potholder and pin in place, forming mitered corners. Edgestitch, using matching thread.

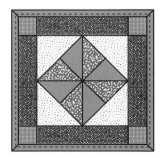

Edgestitch binding.

Starburst Potholder
Foundation Piecing Template

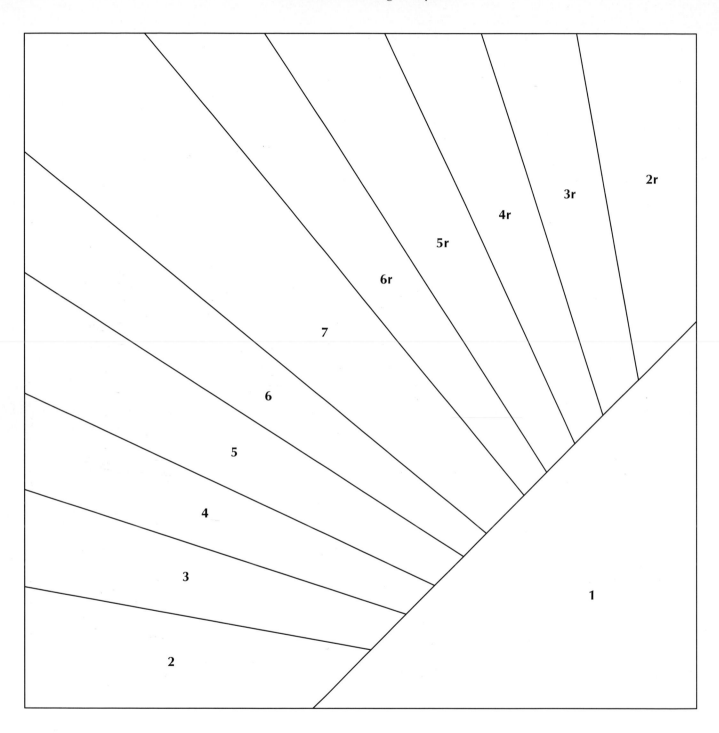

Holiday Splendor

By Mary Lynn Konyu

Holiday Splendor by Mary Lynn Konyu, 1995, Kennewick, Washington, 38^{1}/$_{4}$" x 38^{1}/$_{4}$".

MARY LYNN KONYU

BORN IN ARIZONA, MARY LYNN EX-PERIENCED A SERIES OF FREQUENT MOVES THROUGHOUT CHILDHOOD. AT AGE TEN, SHE PICKED UP THE NEEDLE HER MOTHER GAVE HER, AND NEEDLEWORK HAS BEEN A SOURCE OF PLEASURE EVER SINCE. IT WAS EASY TO TAKE ALONG AS THE FAMILY MOVED FROM TOWN TO TOWN, AND IT INSTIGATED FRIENDSHIPS AND CONNECTIONS WITH OTHER "FABRIHOLICS." MARY LYNN'S FOCUS SHIFTED TO QUILTMAKING IN 1989 WHEN A CHRISTMAS TREE SKIRT SHE HAD TO HAVE INSPIRED HER TO TAKE SOME QUILT-ING CLASSES. IT WAS LOVE AT FIRST STITCH!

MARY LYNN BEGAN TEACHING AT QUILT SHOPS IN 1992 AND CREDITS HER CO-WORKERS, FRIENDS, AND EMPLOYERS WITH SHARING THEIR EXPERTISE AND PROVIDING THE ENCOURAGEMENT TO MOVE BEYOND THE REALM OF "TECH-NICIAN" AND DIVE INTO CREATING.

A BUSY MOTHER OF THREE SONS, MARY LYNN IS ACTIVE IN HER COMMUNITY, HER CHURCH, AND THE BOY SCOUTS OF AMERICA. SHE IS A MEMBER OF THE WASH-INGTON STATE QUILTERS, SOUTH BAY QUILTERS (TORRANCE, CALIFORNIA), AND SHE IS CURRENTLY PRESIDENT OF THE SOUTH EASTERN WASHINGTON GUILD IN KENNEWICK, WASHINGTON.

"HOLIDAY SPLENDOR" IS MARY LYNN'S FIRST ORIGINAL DESIGN. THE AIRINESS OF THE FEATHERED STAR HAS ALWAYS HAD AN APPEAL FOR HER, AND SHE JUST "HAD TO" MAKE THIS QUILT. SETTING LITTLE LOG CABIN BLOCKS ON POINT IN THE PIECED OUTER BORDER ADDS MOVEMENT TO THIS LIVELY CHRISTMAS QUILT. MARY LYNN'S HUSBAND USED HIS ENGINEERING SKILLS TO HELP HER DUR-ING THE PROGRESSION FROM TECHNICAL PATTERN DESIGN TO THE RESULTING PERSONAL STATEMENT IN FABRIC.

Quilt Size: 38¼" x 38¼"

Materials: 44"-wide fabric

1 yd. light print for background and outer borders

½ yd. green/red/gold holiday print for star, inner border #2, outer pieced border, and binding

⅛ yd. gold print for Log Cabin centers

⅜ yd. red print #1 for Sawtooth Star center and inner border #1

⅛ yd. red print #2 for Log Cabin blocks

¼ yd. red print #3 for Log Cabin blocks

⅝ yd. green print #1 for Feathered Star block and binding

⅛ yd. green print #2 for Log Cabin blocks

¼ yd. green print #3 for Log Cabin blocks

¼ yd. green print #4 for Log Cabin blocks

Cutting and Piecing

Sawtooth Star Center

1. Cut the required pieces, referring to the chart below. *Cut all strips across the fabric width (crosswise grain).* Crosscut each strip into the required pieces. Label all pieces.

Fabric	No. of Strip	Strip Width	No. of Pieces	Dimensions	Piece
Holiday print	1	2½"	4	2½" x 4½"	A
			4	2½" x 2½"	B
				4½" x 4½"	
Red #1	1	4½"	1	4½" x 4½"	C
	1	2½"	8	2½" x 2½"	D

2. Draw a diagonal line on the wrong side of each red 2½" square (D). Place each square on a 2½" x 4½" rectangle of holiday print (A). Stitch on the line and trim ¼" from the stitching. Press toward the resulting triangle corner.

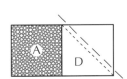
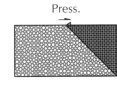

Stitch and trim. Make 4.

3. Add a square to opposite ends of 2 pieced rectangles in the same way. Trim and press.

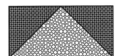

Make 4.

4. Arrange the pieced units in rows with the remaining pieces. Sew the pieces together in rows and press the seams in the direction of the arrows. Sew the rows together.

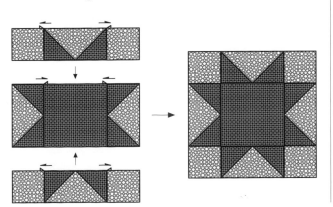

Feathered Star

*You will need the Baby Bias Square®
to make these units.*

1. From the light print background fabric, cut 1 piece, 18" x 22". Set aside for bias strips in step 4 below. Cut 1 square, 11¼" x 11¼". Cut twice diagonally to yield 4 quarter-square triangles (B).

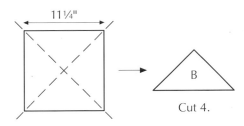

Cut 4.

2. From green print #1, cut 1 piece, 18" x 22". Set aside for bias strips in step 4 below.

3. Cut the remaining pieces, referring to the chart below. *Cut all strips across the fabric width (crosswise grain).* Crosscut each strip into the required pieces. If additional cutting is needed to arrive at the required shape, an asterisk appears with the letter in the "Piece" column, and directions are given in the steps that follow the cutting chart. An "r" next to a letter means you should flip the piece over and cut a reverse image of it. Label all pieces.

Fabric	No. of Strips	Strip Width	No. of Pieces	Dimensions	Piece
Light print	1	6⅛"	4	6⅛" x 6⅛"	A
			4	1⅞" x 1⅞"	C*
			4	2" x 2"	D*
Holiday print	1	4⅞"	4	4⅞" x 4⅞"	E*
Green #1	2	1½"	4 and 4r		H* and Hr*

4. Layer the green and light print 18" x 22" rectangles right sides up. Referring to step 2 in the directions for "Bias Strip–Piecing Method" on pages 120–21, cut 8 bias strips, each 2" wide. You will have a total of 16 strips, 8 of each.

19. Arrange the completed units and sew together in rows. Sew the rows together, beginning and ending the stitching at the seam intersection where the units meet at the outer edges. Then complete the diagonal seams to complete the Feathered Star Medallion. The piece should measure 21³/4" x 21³/4".

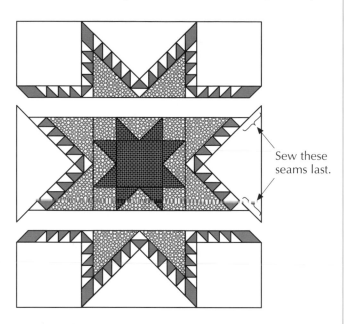

Sew these seams last.

Inner Borders #1 and #2

Note: To cut border strips for the center star, refer to the directions for "Straight-Cut Borders" on page 124. Border-strip dimensions are given below for a medallion that measures 21³/4" x 21³/4", but yours may be a little off.

1. From red print #1, cut 2 strips, each 1¹/2" x 21³/4". Sew to opposite edges of the Feathered Star Medallion. Cut 2 red strips, each 1¹/2" x 24¹/4". Sew to the remaining edges of the medallion.
2. From the holiday print, cut 2 strips, each 1¹/2" x 24¹/4". Sew to opposite edges of the medallion. Cut

2 print strips, 1¹/2" x 26³/4". Sew to the remaining edges of the medallion. The medallion should now measure 25³/4" x 25³/4".

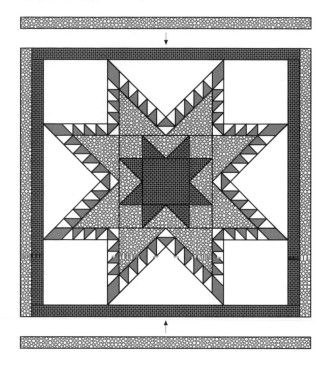

Log Cabin Borders

1. Cut the required number of 1" x 42" strips for the logs.

Fabric	No. of Strips
Red #2	3
Red #3	5
Green #2	2
Green #3	3
Green #4	6

2. Cut the remaining pieces, referring to the chart on page 79. *Cut all strips across the fabric width (crosswise grain).* Crosscut each strip into the required pieces. If additional cutting is required to arrive at the required shape, an asterisk appears with the letter in the "Piece" column, and directions are given in the steps that follow the cutting chart. Label all pieces.

Fabric	No. of Strips	Strip Width	No. of Pieces	Dimensions	Piece
Gold	1	1"	28	1" x 1"	A
Holiday print	1	1⅛"	4	1⅛" x 2⅛"	G
			4	1⅛" x 2⅝"	H
	1	5½"	5	5½" x 5½"	O*
		3"	4	3" x 3"	P*
Light print	1	1⅛"	4	1⅛" x 3½"	I
			4	1⅛" x 4⅛"	J
			4	1⅛" x 2½"	K
			4	1⅛" x 2⅝"	L
	1	5½"	5	5½" x 5½"	M*
		3"	4	3" x 3"	N*

3. Place each gold square (A) face down on a strip of green print #2 and chain-piece, stitching ¼" from the raw edge and leaving a little space between each one. Cut apart and press the seam toward the green square (B) in each unit.

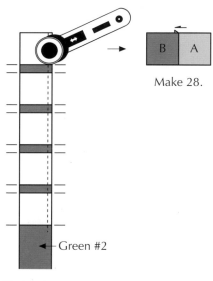

Make 28.

Chain-piece.
Cut apart.

4. Rotate the unit so the gold square is at the top and chain-piece to the right side of a green print #2

strip. Cut apart and press the seam toward the green rectangle (B).

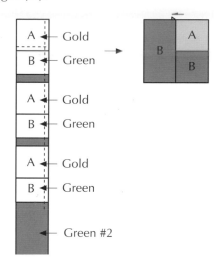

5. Rotate the unit counterclockwise and place on a strip of red print #2. Chain-piece, cut apart, and press the seam toward the red rectangle.

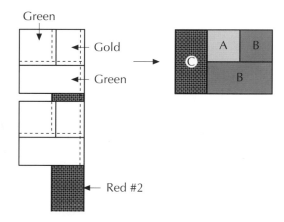

6. Continuing to rotate the unit counterclockwise for each new log, add 1 more round of red print #2, then 2 rounds of green print #3, 2 rounds of red print #3, and 2 rounds of green print #4. The finished block should measure 3½" x 3½".

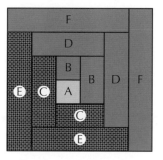

Make 28.

7. Sew the remaining rectangles of light print (I and J) to 4 of the Log Cabin blocks.

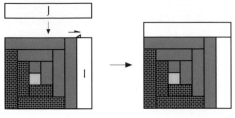

Make 4.

8. Sew the 4 rectangles of holiday print (G and H) and the 4 light print rectangles (K and L) together as shown.

Make 4.   Make 4.

9. Assemble the 4 corner Log Cabin blocks as shown.

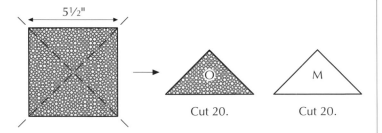

Make 4.

10. Cut the 5½" squares of holiday print and light print twice diagonally to make 20 quarter-square triangles (O and M) of each (40 total).

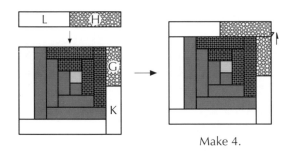

Cut 20.   Cut 20.

11. Cut the 3" squares of holiday print and light print once diagonally to yield 8 half-square triangles (P and N) of each (16 total).

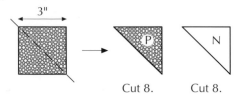

Cut 8.   Cut 8.

12. To assemble the pieced border strips, arrange the light print and holiday print triangles with the Log Cabin blocks to make 4 identical rows. Sew together in diagonal rows. Sew the rows together, adding the corner triangles (N and P) last.

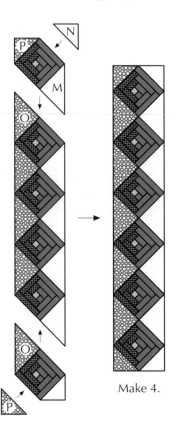

Make 4.

13. Sew a pieced border strip to opposite sides of the quilt top.

14. Add a corner Log Cabin block to opposite ends of the 2 remaining pieced border strips. Sew to the top and bottom edges of the quilt top. Refer to the quilt plan on page 74.

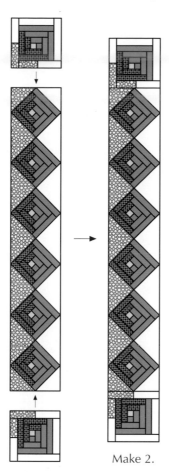

Make 2.

Outer Border

1. From the remaining light print, cut 4 strips, each 2¼" x 42".
2. Referring to the directions for "Straight-Cut Borders" on page 124, measure the quilt for side borders, cut the strips to fit, and sew to opposite sides of the quilt top. Repeat for the top and bottom borders.

Finishing

Refer to pages 124–28 to finish your quilt.

1. Mark the quilt top with the desired quilting pattern or follow the quilting suggestion below.
2. Layer the quilt top with batting and backing; baste.
3. Quilt on the marked lines.
4. Add a hanging sleeve if desired.
5. Bind the edges with double-fold binding, using 2½"-wide straight-grain strips cut from the remaining holiday print.
6. Sign your quilt.

S~A~N~T~A

By Tonee White

S-A-N-T-A by Tonee White, 1995, Irvine, California, 17" x 50".

TONEE WHITE

TONEE BEGAN QUILTING SIX YEARS AGO OUT OF A LOVE FOR QUILTS AND A LACK OF FUNDS TO BUY AS MANY QUILTS AS SHE WOULD LIKE TO OWN. SHE TOOK HER FIRST CLASS AND, LIKE MANY COMPULSIVE QUILTERS, WAS BITTEN BY THE QUILTING BUG. AS A RESULT, QUILTMAKING HAS BECOME AN ALL-CONSUMING PASSION FOR TONEE. HER FIRST BOOK, *APPLIQUILT®: WHIMSICAL ONE-STEP APPLIQUÉ AND QUILTING*, INTRODUCED QUILTMAKERS TO A QUICK AND EASY WAY TO MAKE APPLIQUÉ QUILTS WITH A PRIMITIVE LOOK. SINCE THEN, SHE HAS WRITTEN TWO MORE BOOKS ON THE SUBJECT FOR THAT PATCHWORK PLACE AND IS BUSY AT WORK ON HER FOURTH ONE. SHE IS ALSO DEVELOPING PROJECTS FOR MORE BOOKS AS WELL AS THE CLASSES AND LECTURES THAT SHE GIVES EXTENSIVELY THROUGHOUT THE COUNTRY.

TONEE LIVES IN SOUTHERN CALIFORNIA WITH HER HUSBAND, BOB, AND FOUR OF HER SEVEN CHILDREN. SHE TRIES TO SPEND AS MUCH TIME AS SHE CAN WITH HER FOUR GRANDCHILDREN.

THE "S-A-N-T-A" WALL HANGING GREW OUT OF TWO OF TONEE'S LOVES: CHRISTMAS AND THE ALPHABET, THE SUBJECTS OF TWO OF HER APPLIQUILT BOOKS. EACH BLOCK DEPICTS TRADITIONAL HOLIDAY MOTIFS TO REPRESENT THE LETTERS THAT SPELL OUT "S-A-N-T-A."

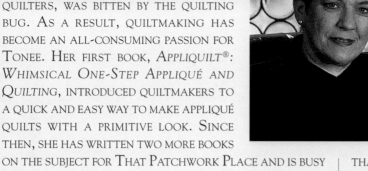

Quilt Size: 17" x 50"

Materials: 44"-wide fabric

Scraps of assorted reds, greens, blues, golds, browns, beiges, whites, white flannel, and batting

1/3 yd. light print for background

1/3 yd. red-and-green print for border

3/4 yd. fabric for backing (or 1 1/2 yds. for unpieced backing)

3/4 yd. thin polyester fleece (or 1 1/2 yds. for unpieced fleece)

Optional: Buttons, bells, ribbon, and assorted embellishments

Black permanent marking pen

Embroidery floss, #8 perle cotton, or topstitching thread in assorted colors

Pinking shears

Appliquilt® Stitching

Appliquilt is a method for appliquéing and quilting design shapes to a quilt top that is already sandwiched with backing and batting. You use pinking shears to cut out the shapes, and you usually do not turn under edges as you hand stitch the appliqués in place.

The stitching is the most important ingredient in any Appliquilt project, and happily, it is the easiest to do. It is important to relax and have fun. Don't worry about the size and uniformity of your stitches. The larger and more uneven they are, the more primitive your piece will look. Don't bury those knots in the batting. Allow them to sit proudly on top for all to see. This also adds to the primitive look.

- Use #8 perle cotton or 3 to 4 strands of embroidery floss and a size 6 or 7 embroidery needle. Moisten and flatten the cotton or floss ends to make them easier to thread through the eye of the needle. The smaller the needle, the easier it is to pull it through all the quilt layers.
- Start stitching on the top side of your quilt, leaving a 6"-long tail of thread. Using a simple running or basting stitch, sew through all layers.
- If you are stitching around a large piece or along a continuous line and run out of perle cotton or embroidery floss, end your stitching on top and leave a 6"-long tail. Start stitching where you ended, leaving another 6"-long tail. After you have taken a few stitches, tie the two tails together in a secure square knot.

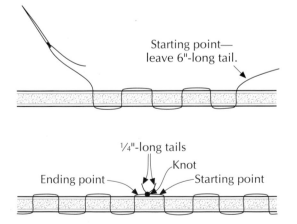

Starting point—leave 6"-long tail.

¼"-long tails
Knot
Ending point
Starting point

- If you begin stitching at a point that you will not return to eventually, tie a knot in the end of your thread before you begin. Start your stitching on the top of your project. When you come to the end of your stitching, gather your last few stitches ever so slightly. Make a loop with your thread and put your needle through the loop, with the tip of your needle resting on the spot where the knot will be. Pull the loop to tighten the knot to the point where the tip of your needle lies. Smooth out the gathers; the knot should sit snugly against the fabric.

- To attach buttons, start stitching on top and leave a 6"-long tail. Take the needle through one hole, down through all layers, then back up through the second hole. Tie off on the top, using a square knot. Clip the ends, leaving little tails.

Note: I embellish most of my projects using a "planned scatter" method. That is, you plan the placement to make it look scattered. Strive for asymmetrical, yet balanced placement.

Cutting

Cut all strips across the width of your fabric (approximately 42").

From the light print, cut:

1 strip, 11½" wide, for the background behind the blocks

From the red-and-green print, cut:

2 strips, each 4" wide, for the side and top borders

1 strip, 3" wide, for the bottom border

Making the Quilt Sandwich

1. Cut the backing and polyester fleece in half along the lengthwise fold.

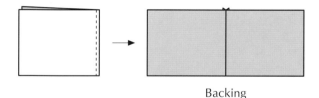

2. With right sides together, sew the backing pieces together along the short end. Press the seam open. Butt the edges of the fleece; zigzag them together.

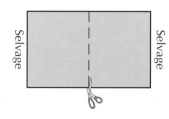

Backing

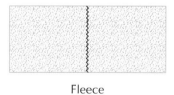

Fleece

3. Lay the backing fabric right side down and place the fleece on top, aligning the raw edges. Smooth out any wrinkles.

4. Position the background piece on top of the fleece, right side up, placing it 6" from the top edge and centering it between the side edges.

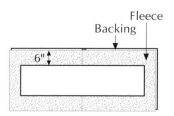

5. Place a 4"-wide border strip, right side down, at the top edge of the background with raw edges even. Pin in place.

6. Place the 3"-wide border strip, right side down, at the bottom edge of the background with raw edges even. Pin in place.

7. Using a ¼"-wide seam allowance, machine stitch borders in place through all layers.

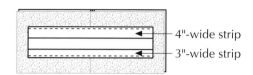

Stitch top and bottom borders to background through all layers.

8. Flip the border pieces open onto the fleece and press toward the outside edge along the seam lines.

9. Cut the remaining 4"-wide border strip into 2 pieces, each 4" x 18". Position each border strip, right side down, on top of the background with raw edges even. Pin in place. Stitch, flip, and press as directed for the top and bottom borders.

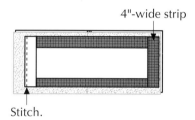

10. *Trim the fleece only*, even with the outer edges of the border. Using pinking shears, trim the backing ¾" from the fleece/border edges.

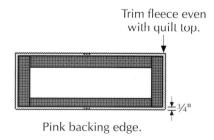

Pink backing edge.

11. Turn the pinked edge over the edge of the fleece and background, mitering the corners. Stitch in place, using a running stitch with embroidery floss or perle cotton. Take 2 stitches across each mitered corner.

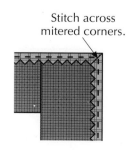

Piecing the Alphabet Blocks

1. Cut the pieces for each of the alphabet-block backgrounds, referring to the illustrations for size and placement.
2. Sew together the pieces for each block in numerical order. Each block should measure 6½" x 6½". Add borders to each block in alphabetical order.

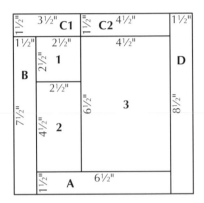

Santa Block

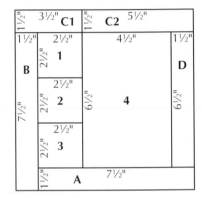

Angel Block

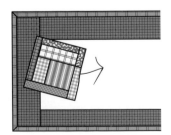

North Pole Block

Tree Block

Antlers Block

3. Arrange the completed blocks on top of the background, referring to the quilt photo on page 82 for placement.
4. Using the tip of your needle, turn under ¼" along the outer edges of each block. Stitch in place through all layers, using a blind stitch. As an alternative to turning the edges, you can pink the block edges, then stitch them to the quilt sandwich without turning under the raw edges.

Turn under edge
with point of needle.

5. Using perle cotton or embroidery floss, hand quilt ⅛" or ¼" inside the edges of all seams.

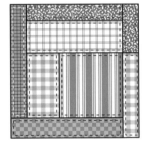

Adding the Appliqués

Use the pattern pieces on pages 89–91 and the pullout.

1. Trace each pattern piece for each block onto template plastic and cut out.
2. Place each pattern piece, *right side down, on the wrong side of the desired fabric*; trace around the outer edge with a pencil.

Note: Refer to the individual block directions that follow for additional information.

3. Use pinking shears to cut the pieces from the fabric along the traced lines.
4. Pin the appliqués in place on the appropriate letter blocks. Refer to block illustrations on page 83.
5. Stitch the appliqués in place in numerical order, using a running stitch and stitching through all layers. Add the desired embellishments.
6. Make 3 white yo-yos, following the directions in the sidebar on page 88.
7. Using the yo-yos and the 3 "H" appliqué pieces, and referring to the quilt photo on page 82 for placement, spell out "HO HO HO" on the border. Stitch in place.

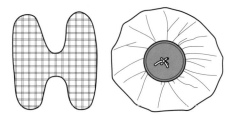

8. Make templates for the roofs and chimneys. Trace on the desired fabrics and cut out with pinking shears.
9. Position the roof and chimney pieces along the bottom border in numerical order, beginning at the lower left corner. Stitch in place, using a running stitch that goes through all layers.

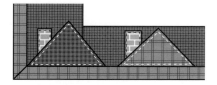

10. Hand quilt wandering lines of stitching that go up from the chimneys between the S-A-N-T-A blocks to emulate smoke rising.

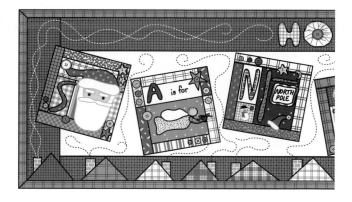

S is for Santa

- Cut the beard and mustache from batting.
- Use white flannel for the hat brim.

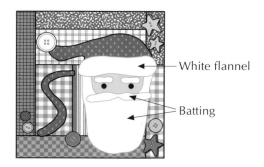

White flannel

Batting

A is for Angel

- Tie 7 knots of perle cotton or embroidery floss on the angel's head as indicated by the dots on the pattern. Sew 3 small bells to the angel's hand, using a 6" length of 1/8"-wide satin ribbon.

Jingle bells

- Stitch "is for" with 3 strands of floss, using a backstitch.

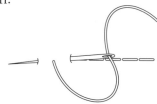

N is for the North Pole

- Trace "NORTH POLE" onto the muslin sign, using a black permanent marking pen.

T is for Tree

- Using pinking shears, cut a 22"-long strip of fabric for the tree. Cut the strip so one end is 1⅛" wide, tapering gradually to ½" at the opposite end.
- Arrange and pin the strip to the block, beginning at the bottom with the widest end of the tree strip and folding it back and forth, narrowing toward the top. Secure the folds with buttons.

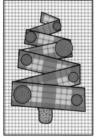

A is for Antlers

- Because the antler patterns are so small, it is better to cut them out with regular scissors.
- Attach a ⅜" x 1¼" piece of ribbon (or a fabric strip of the same dimensions) across the reindeer nose with 3 buttons.

Making Yo-yos

Yo-yos are a wonderful addition to primitive projects and are easy to make using the method below.

1. Draw a 5½"-diameter circle on the wrong side of the fabric. Cut out the circle with pinking shears.
2. Thread a needle with an 18" length of perle cotton or embroidery floss. Make a knot approximately 4" from the end of the thread.
3. With the right side of the fabric facing you, stitch around the circle, ¼" from the outer edge, gathering the fabric against the knot as you stitch.
4. When you have stitched entirely around the circle, adjust the gathers. Do not pull the gathers together entirely. I leave a center hole about the size of my index finger. Tie your thread in a square knot with the tail you left when you started. Flatten the yo-yo with the hole in the center. *Do not remove your needle.*

5. Position the yo-yo on the quilt. With one stitch, sew the yo-yo in position on your quilt, ending the stitching on top. Bring the needle through a hole in a button on top of the yo-yo and sew the button in place, ending your stitching on top. Clip the thread, leaving a 4" tail. Thread the needle with the tail left by the square knot in step 4. Bring it up through the other hole and tie the two tails in a square knot. Clip the ends.

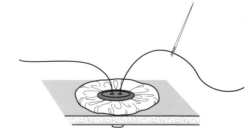

Appliqué Templates
*Cut 1 of each piece unless
otherwise indicated.*

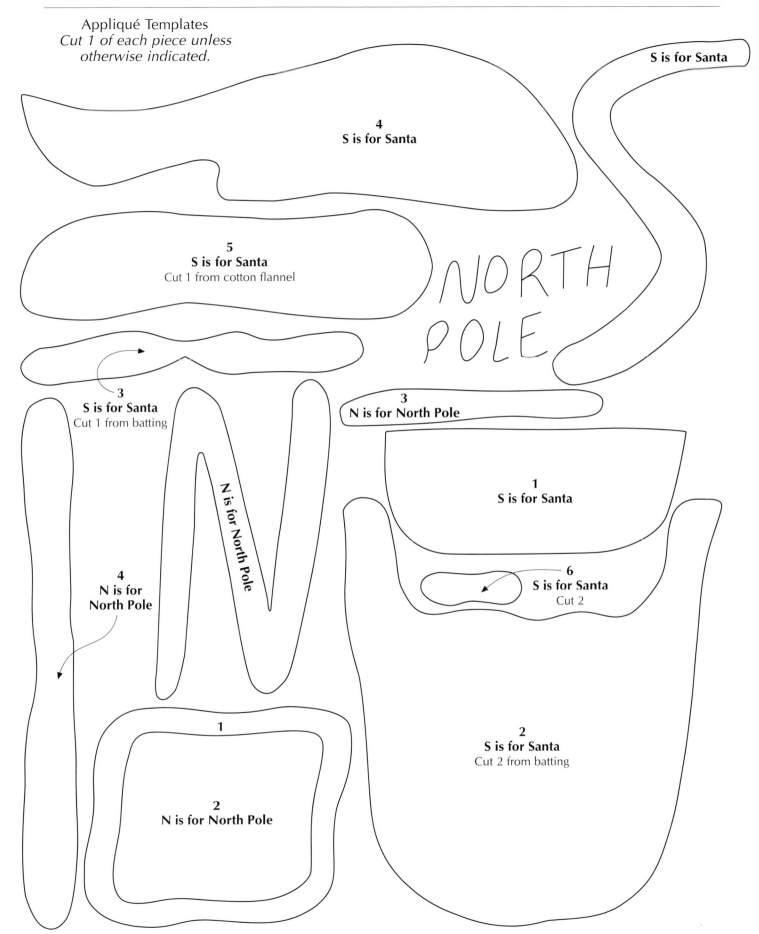

S is for Santa

4
S is for Santa

NORTH POLE

5
S is for Santa
Cut 1 from cotton flannel

3
S is for Santa
Cut 1 from batting

3
N is for North Pole

N is for North Pole

1
S is for Santa

4
**N is for
North Pole**

6
S is for Santa
Cut 2

1

2
N is for North Pole

2
S is for Santa
Cut 2 from batting

Gilded Stocking

By Melody Crust

Gilded Stocking by Melody Crust, 1994, Kent, Washington, 10" x 20".

MELODY CRUST

MELODY IS A MULTIFACETED QUILTER WHOSE LOVE OF FABRIC IS REFLECTED IN HER DESIGNING AND TEACHING. HER PROFOUND BELIEF IN "THE QUILT AS ART" HAS MOTIVATED HER TO INITIATE SEVERAL QUILT-ART PROMOTIONAL ACTIVITIES. AN ACTIVE MEMBER OF THREE QUILT GUILDS, MELODY CO-FOUNDED AND IS VICE PRESIDENT OF THE ASSOCIATION OF PACIFIC NORTHWEST QUILTERS (APNQ). IN 1994, APNQ PRODUCED THE FIRST JUDGED AND JURIED QUILT EXHIBITION IN THEIR AREA.

MELODY'S QUILTS EXPRESS DIVERSE THEMES—SOME ABSTRACT, SOME PICTORIAL—WITH AND WITHOUT EMBELLISHMENT. SHE IS FASCINATED AND INSPIRED BY THE GLORIES OF NATURE AND THE INTERPLAY OF COLORS AND TEXTURES. USING A RICH VARIETY OF FABRICS, MELODY ENJOYS THE CHALLENGE OF TRANSLATING HER CREATIVE VISION INTO FABRIC, AND SHE LOVES TO "GILD" HER WORK WITH EMBELLISHMENTS. MELODY'S ART QUILTS ARE EXHIBITED INTERNATIONALLY AND ARE FREQUENT AWARD WINNERS. MUCH OF HER WORK IS IN PRIVATE COLLECTIONS AND HAS BEEN PUBLISHED IN QUILTING BOOKS AND MAGAZINES. HER QUILTS ARE AVAILABLE AT TWO GALLERIES IN THE WESTERN PART OF THE UNITED STATES .

THIS ELABORATE STOCKING REFLECTS MELODY'S LOVE OF EMBROIDERY AND EMBELLISHMENT. SHE CREATED THE CRAZY QUILT DESIGN IN AN EFFORT TO USE TREASURES FROM HER COLLECTION OF FABRICS, BUTTONS, BEADS, AND THREADS. IT WAS A PERFECT PROJECT TO CARRY WITH HER WHILE SHE TRAVELED WITH HER PHOTOGRAPHER HUSBAND.

Stocking Size: 10" x 20"

Materials and Supplies

Scraps of red fabrics in a variety of weaves and fiber contents: satin, silk, lame, moiré, and cotton in an assortment of prints, solids, and textures, including at least one fairly dark, solid-colored fabric

12" x 22" piece of muslin

1/2 yd. moiré or other fancy medium- to heavyweight fabric for the stocking back and lining

10" x 40" piece of woven fusible interfacing

10" x 40" piece of polyester fleece or thin cotton batting

Nymo thread (nylon beading thread)

6 yds. red rattail cord

8"-long piece of red fringe

16" x 22" piece of cardboard for window template

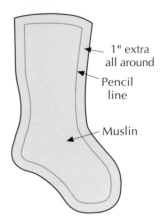

stocking foundation. Cut 1 stocking, adding an extra 1" all around.

1" extra
all around

Pencil
line

Muslin

Embellishments

*Variety is the spice of life; choose some
or all of the following:*

Embroidery floss, silk buttonhole twist, and metallic threads in assorted colors that contrast with the fabrics

Assorted beads, buttons, and brass charms

Pieces from old jewelry

Scraps of ribbon in assorted styles (picot-edged, satin, grosgrain, velvet) from 1/16" to 3/8" wide

Assorted decorative scraps

Lace scraps or lace motifs

Assembling the Stocking

Use the pattern on the pullout.

1. Trace the stocking pattern onto cardboard and cut the shape out of the cardboard to create a window template. Discard the center cutout.

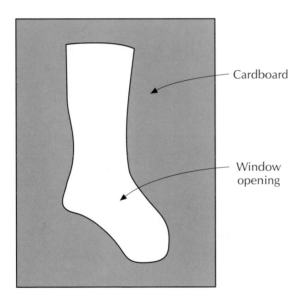

Cardboard

Window
opening

2. Place the window template on the muslin and draw along the inner edge of the window. This is the

3. Use the window template to mark and cut 2 stockings from fleece and 2 from the fusible interfacing. Cut 3 stockings from the moiré, reversing 1. Add a 1/4"-wide seam allowance all around on each piece before cutting.

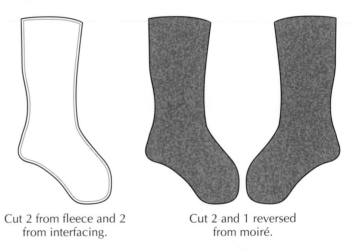

Cut 2 from fleece and 2
from interfacing.

Cut 2 and 1 reversed
from moiré.

4. From the dark solid, cut a 2" to 3" five-sided piece. Position the piece right side up on the right side of the muslin foundation, approximately in the center. Pin in place.

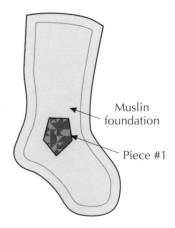

Muslin
foundation

Piece #1

5. From the next fabric, cut a rectangle, approximately 3" x 5", to match the length of one edge of piece #1. Position the rectangle face down with raw edges even on top of piece #1. Stitch ¼" from the raw edges. Use a long stitch. After stitching, flip the second rectangle over and check the fit. If necessary, remove a few stitches and restitch.

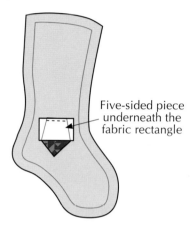

Five-sided piece underneath the fabric rectangle

Trim the seam allowances to ⅛", then turn the rectangle back onto the muslin foundation and press carefully.

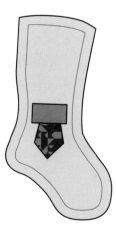

6. From the next fabric, cut a rectangle long enough to match the length of pieces #1 and #2, working in a clockwise direction. Position the rectangle face down with raw edges even on top of pieces #1 and

#2. Stitch ¼" from the raw edges and trim the seam allowances to ⅛". Turn the rectangle onto the foundation and press carefully.

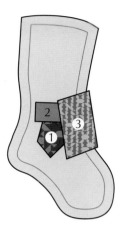

7. Continue cutting and adding rectangles to the remaining edges of piece #1 in the same fashion. Remember that each rectangle must be long enough to cover the edge of the center piece and those already added to it. After adding 5 rectangles, trim the excess to create new angles; continue adding pieces in the same manner until the foundation is covered. As you position the pieces, pay careful attention to color and texture placement for good balance.

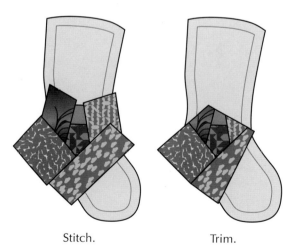

Stitch.   Trim.

8. Place the window template on top of the foundation and draw around the inner edges with a marking pencil or chalk. Remove the template and

cut out, adding a 1/4"-wide seam allowance all around. Staystitch 1/8" from the raw edges.

Staystitch 1/8" from raw edges.

9. Add embellishments as desired, referring to the stocking photo for ideas and to "Gilding Tips" below. Add embroidery and/or ribbon, lace, or trim to each seam; then add beads, buttons, and charms as desired. See "Embroidery Stitches" on page 97 and "Ribbon Roses" on page 15.

Gilding Tips

- Variety is the spice of embellishment.
- If the stocking doesn't look "finished," it's not; add more embellishment.
- Couch ribbon or trims in place over seam lines, using fancy stitches and thread to anchor them in place.
- Use beads to fasten twisted or flat ribbon, to accent stitches, to accent the fabric design, or as flower centers.
- Buttons look better when added in groups of uneven numbers.
- Sew on buttons with contrasting thread. Or, stack buttons or add beads on top of buttons.

Finishing

1. Following the manufacturer's directions, apply interfacing to the wrong side of 2 lining pieces.

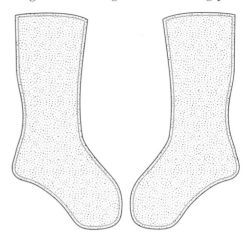

Apply fusible interfacing to 2 lining pieces.

2. Place the embellished stocking face down on the right side of one of the interfaced lining pieces. Place the batting stocking on top. Pin the layers together. Stitch 1/4" from the raw edges, leaving a 3"-long opening on the long side.

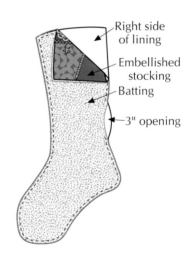

Right side of lining

Embellished stocking

Batting

3" opening

3. Trim the seam to 1/8". Turn the stocking right side out through the opening, press carefully, and whipstitch the opening edges together. Hand sew or machine stitch fringe to the top edge of the stocking front.

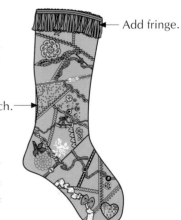

Add fringe.

Whipstitch.

4. Repeat steps 2 and 3 with the remaining batting and lining pieces, disregarding the reference to fringe.

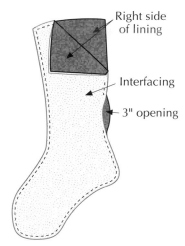

Right side of lining

Interfacing

3" opening

5. Cut a 10"-long piece from the rattail cord and set aside. Cut the remaining cord into 3 equal lengths, then braid together, leaving the first and last 6" to 8" unbraided. Tie a knot at the end of each piece.

6" to 8"   6" to 8"

6. Hand baste the 2 finished stocking pieces together. Beginning at the upper corner of the long edge of the stocking, hand couch the braided cord to the outer edge of the stocking, catching both layers of the stocking in the stitching. Attach braid to the upper opening edge of the stocking front only.

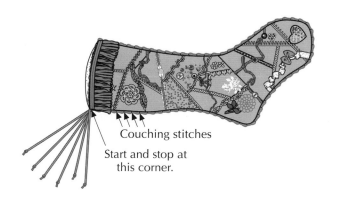

Couching stitches

Start and stop at this corner.

7. Gather the cord ends together at the corner and place the 10" length of cord alongside with ends even. Make a loop and tightly wrap the cord around the gathered cord 6 to 8 times. Start wrapping from the ends and work toward the stocking. Bring the cord end through the loop and pull hard on the opposite end. Trim excess cord and knot the end.

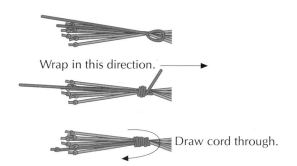

Wrap in this direction.

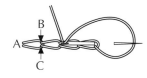

Draw cord through.

Embroidery Stitches

Bring thread up at A, leave small loop, then down at A. Come up at B, then pass needle through loop, and down at C. Start new stitch.

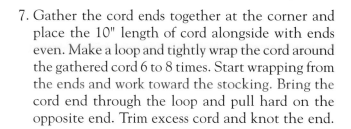

Chain Stitch

Work the same as chain stitch A, but fasten each loop at the center with small stitch B. May be worked singly or in groups.

Lazy Daisy Stitch

Bring up at A, down at B, up at C.

Chevron Stitch

Bring needle up at A. Holding the thread under your left thumb, go down at B and up at C. Variation: Stitch twice with different-colored threads.

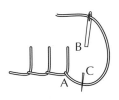

Blanket Stitch

Basket of Roses

By Bonnie Kaster

Basket of Roses by Bonnie Kaster, 1995, DePere, Wisconsin, 24" x 29".

BONNIE KASTER

BONNIE HAS BEEN QUILTING FOR ABOUT FOURTEEN YEARS. EARLY IN HER CAREER, SHE PARTICIPATED IN A FEW CLASSES, THEN DECIDED TO CONCENTRATE ON THE TECHNIQUES THAT WERE OF MOST INTEREST TO HER. WITH A BACKGROUND IN ART AND FASHION, BONNIE BEGAN DESIGNING ORIGINAL QUILTED JACKETS AND VESTS ABOUT TWELVE YEARS AGO. SHE HAS WON MANY AWARDS FOR HER WORK, INCLUDING THE STAFF'S CHOICE AWARD IN THE 1992 KEEPSAKE QUILTING CHALLENGE. SHE WAS A FINALIST IN A CONTEST SPONSORED BY GOOD HOUSEKEEPING AND ALSO WON AN AWARD IN THE FLORAL GARDENS CONTEST HOSTED BY

CREATIVE QUILTING IN 1991. IN 1992, BONNIE AND HER PARTNER, VIRGINIA ATHEY, BEGAN PRODUCING AND PUBLISHING A LINE OF QUILT PATTERNS UNDER THE NAME "SWEET MEMORIES." BONNIE LIVES WITH HER HUSBAND AND THREE CHILDREN IN DE PERE, WISCONSIN.

BONNIE DESIGNED "BASKET OF ROSES" IN THE SPRING OF 1995 FOR THIS BOOK. SHE WAS IN A CHRISTMAS MOOD AND WANTED TO DO SOMETHING FLORAL BUT WAS TIRED OF POINSETTIAS. SINCE SHE HAS ALWAYS ENJOYED RED ROSES FOR CHRISTMAS, IT WAS ONLY NATURAL TO THINK OF PLACING THEM IN A BASKET WITH PLENTY OF HOLLY AND ORNATE GOLD BALLS.

Quilt Size: 24" x 29"

Materials: 44"-wide fabric

5/8 yd. light tan print for center background

1/3 yd. gold print for basket

1/3 yd. brown print for basket handle, base, and rim

1/3 yd. dark green print #1 for outer border, holly stems and some leaves, and inner parts of bow

1/4 yd. dark green print #2 for remaining holly leaves

1/3 yd. red plaid for ribbon and bow

1/4 yd. gold metallic for Christmas balls

1/8 yd. each of very dark, medium, and light red solids or prints for roses and berries*

1/3 yd. medium tan print for outer border

1/3 yd. Christmas print for outer border

1/8 yd. medium red solid for inner border

1 yd. for backing

28" x 33" piece of low-loft batting

1/4 yd. dark green print for binding

Thread to match appliqué fabrics

*If desired, use scraps of synthetic suede, such as Ultra Suede®, for the berries.

Cutting

Use the templates on the pullout pattern. Cut and prepare all appliqué shapes, using your favorite appliqué method. (See pages 121–23.) Use your rotary equipment to cut the center panel, border, and binding strips.

From the light tan print, cut:
1 piece, 18" x 23", for the center panel
From the gold print, cut:
1 of basket 1
From the brown print, cut:
1 each of baskets 2, 3, and 4
From dark green print #1, cut:
1 each of stems 1–4
1 each of holly leaves 2, 4, 5, 7, 8, and 11
1 each of R1, R2A, R5A, R6A, and R8A for the bow
4 border holly leaves
2 each of outer border Templates #4 and #5
From dark green print #2, cut:
1 each of holly leaves 1, 3, 6, 9, and 10
4 border holly leaves
From the red plaid fabric, cut:
1 each of the right and left ribbon streamers
1 each of R2–R9 for the bow
From the gold metallic fabric, cut:
1 each of balls 1–4
From the medium red solids or prints, cut:
24 berries
From the medium red solid for inner border, cut:
2 strips, each ³⁄₄" x 21³⁄₄"
2 strips, each 1" x 17³⁄₄"
From the medium tan print, cut:
8 outer border corners (Template #1)
From the Christmas print, cut:
2 each of outer border Templates #2 and #3

Note: To cut the pieces for the roses, see the sidebar, "Cutting and Assembling the Roses," at right.

Cutting and Assembling the Roses

1. From dark red fabric, cut 2 each of rose 1 and rose 2.
2. From the medium red fabric, cut 4 of rose Template F.
3. To begin each rose, tuck a piece F under a base and appliqué the base to it.

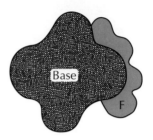

4. Cut the remaining rose petals for each rose from assorted red fabrics. Refer to the pullout pattern for the correct petal shapes and correct placement for each. Appliqué the petals to each base. The base color should show through in the spaces around the petals, creating a realistic look. (The shaded areas represent the base of each rose.)

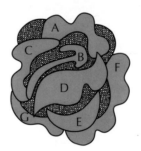

Rose 1   Rose 2

5. Set aside for step 17 on page 102.

Appliquéing the Center Panel

*Refer to the pullout pattern for positioning each
numbered piece as directed below.*

1. Lightly trace the basket design onto the 18" x 23" center panel.
2. Baste the basket handle and basket (B1) to the center panel.
3. Position and pin stems S1, S2, S3, and S4 along the basket handle, tucking the ends under the handle where shown.
4. Position and baste holly pieces 6, 7, 8, 9, and 11 to the center panel.
5. Appliqué all basted pieces in place. Remove the basting.

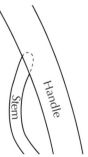

6. Position holly pieces 5 and 10 and the left and right ribbon streamers; baste in place.
7. Position basket 3 under the bottom edge of basket 1 and appliqué.

8. Position basket 2 along the top edge of basket 1 and appliqué the bottom edge only.
9. Position balls 1–4, tucking 3 and 4 under the top edge of basket 2. Baste in place.

10. Position and appliqué bow pieces 1–9 in numerical order.
11. Appliqué holly pieces 5 and 10.
12. Position ribbon 10, tucking it behind ball 2. Appliqué.
13. Appliqué the right and left ribbons.
14. Position holly 4 and baste in place. Appliqué.

15. Appliqué the top edge of basket 2.
16. Position, baste, and appliqué holly 1, 2, and 3.
17. Baste the roses in place, tucking them behind balls 3 and 4. Appliqué.

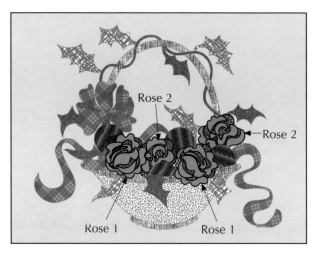

Rose 2 (far right) is tucked behind ball 4.
Rose 2 (second from left) is tucked behind ball 3.
Rose 1 (far left) is appliquéd over ball 1.
Rose 1 (second from right) is appliquéd over balls 2, 3, and 4.

18. Appliqué holly berries along the stem.
19. Appliqué all remaining loose pieces. Remove all basting.
20. Press the center panel, being very careful not to put the hot iron on the metallic-fabric balls.
21. Trim the center panel to 16¾" x 21¾", being careful to keep the appliquéd design centered in the panel.

Adding the Borders

1. Sew a medium red ¾" x 21¾" strip to the top and bottom edges of the center panel. Press the seams toward the center panel. Sew the remaining medium red strips to the sides of the quilt top.
2. Assemble the pieced outer borders, pressing the long seams toward the green strips and the short seams toward the trapezoids.

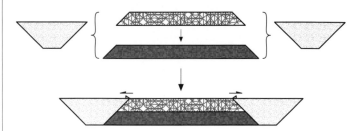

Top and Bottom Borders

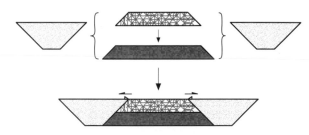

Side Borders

3. Sew each pieced border to the quilt top, beginning and ending the stitching ¼" from the quilt-top corner edge.

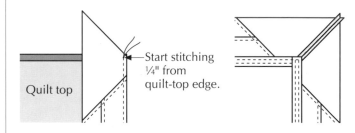

Quilt top

Start stitching ¼" from quilt-top edge.

4. Complete each mitered corner and press the seam open.
5. Position and appliqué holly leaves and berries in the corner of each border.

Finishing

Refer to pages 124–28 to finish your quilt.

1. Layer the quilt top with batting and backing; baste.
2. Quilt as desired or follow the quilting suggestion below. I quilted diagonally across the background, spacing rows either ½" or 1" apart and ending at the appliqués. I also quilted around the outer edge of each appliqué.
3. Add a hanging sleeve if desired.
4. Bind the edges of the quilt with 1¼"-wide straight-grain strips of dark green fabric, using a ¼"-wide seam allowance.
5. Sign your quilt.

Light a Little Candle

By Leslie Beck and Retta Warehime

Light a Little Candle by Leslie Beck and Retta Warehime, 1995, Kennewick, Washington, 35" x 41".
Quilted by Vi McDonald.

LESLIE BECK AND RETTA WAREHIME

LESLIE AND RETTA HAVE BEEN FRIENDS FOR A NUMBER OF YEARS, SHARING THEIR LOVE OF QUILTMAKING. THEY EACH DESIGN PROJECTS FOR THEIR OWN PATTERN LINES. IN FACT, RETTA HELPED LESLIE GET HER COMPANY STARTED A FEW YEARS AGO. EACH HAS HER OWN DISTINCT STYLE, YET THEIR STYLES COMPLEMENT EACH OTHER. RETTA'S FORTE IS SPEED PIECING, WHICH REQUIRES ROTARY CUTTING INSTEAD OF TEMPLATES. LESLIE USES NO-SEW APPLIQUÉ TECHNIQUES TO BRING HER WHIMSICAL CHARACTERS TO LIFE. THE TWO FRIENDS OFTEN TALKED ABOUT DESIGNING A QUILT TOGETHER. WHEN THE OPPORTUNITY TO SUBMIT DESIGNS FOR THE THIRD VOLUME OF *QUILTED FOR CHRISTMAS* APPEARED IN THEIR INDIVIDUAL MAIL-BOXES, THEY KNEW IT WAS TIME TO COMBINE THEIR EFFORTS.

"LIGHT A LITTLE CAN-DLE" REFLECTS RETTA AND LESLIE'S WISH THAT EACH OF US WOULD TAKE A MINUTE DURING THE BUSY HOLIDAY SEASON TO BECOME A CHILD AGAIN AND SHARE A SMILE WITH SOMEONE NEW—TO GREET NEIGHBORS, CALL FAMILY FRIENDS, REFLECT ON WARM CHILD-HOOD MEMORIES OF CHRISTMAS SEASONS PAST, AND CREATE OUR OWN TRADITIONS TO SHARE WITH OTHERS.

Quilt Size: 35" x 41"

Materials: 44"-wide fabric

7 different light prints for section backgrounds:
  ⅝ yd. for stars and candles
  ⅜ yd. for 2 small angels
  ⅛ yd. for banner
  ¼ yd. for Christmas tree
  ¼ yd. for wreath
  ⅓ yd. for large angel
  ⅛ yd. for Ohio Star with candle

¼ yd. gold print for large stars

⅛ yd. green for leaves

Scraps of yellow for candle flames

Scraps of 5 different prints for candlesticks

Assorted green, red, blue, brown, tan, white, gold, and burgundy scraps for tree, wreaths, Ohio Star, angels, and patchwork sashing strips

⅛ yd. blue print for banner borders

¼ yd. burgundy print #1 for inner border

½ yd. dark green print for outer border

1⅛ yds. fabric for backing

39" x 45" piece of batting

⅓ yd. burgundy print #2 for binding

Miscellaneous Supplies

1 yd. paper-backed fusible web,
such as HeatnBond®

1/4 yd. fusible interfacing

Sakura Micron pigma pen

Blue water-soluble marking pen

8 buttons, each 1" in diameter, for stars

20 small buttons for tree and patchwork sashing

1 skein black embroidery floss

Cutting and Piecing

Stars

Cut all strips across the fabric width (crosswise grain) for 42"-long strips.

Fabric	No. of Strips	Strip Width	No. of Pieces	Dimensions
Background	5	1½"	48	1½" x 1½"
			24	1½" x 2½"
			7	1½" x 4½"
			1	1" x 4½"
Gold print	3	1½"	16	1½" x 1½"
			16	1½" x 2½"
			8	1½" x 4½"

Angled Piecing

The pieced blocks in this quilt are made from squares and rectangles. To create the triangular shapes and angled seams, use angled piecing.

To sew a small square to a larger square or to a rectangle:

1. Draw a diagonal line on the wrong side of the small square.
2. Lay the small square on the larger square or rectangle right sides together, with the diagonal line lying in the direction indicated in the illustrations for the block you are piecing.

3. Stitch on the diagonal line and cut away the excess fabric, leaving a 1/4"-wide seam allowance. (If you prefer, cut away the excess on the small block only.) Press seam allowances toward the darker fabric, unless otherwise directed.

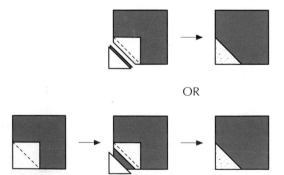

OR

Note: When sewing two or more squares to another piece of fabric, add one square, cut away the excess, and press. Then repeat until you've added all the squares.

To sew a rectangle to a rectangle:

1. With right sides together, lay one rectangle on top of another at a 90° angle, matching corners. Draw a line at a 45° angle from the corner of the top rectangle to the corner of the bottom rectangle.

2. Stitch along the diagonal line and cut away excess fabric, leaving a 1/4"-wide seam allowance. Press seam allowances toward the dark fabric unless otherwise directed.

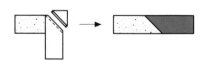

Note: For a rectangle with an angled seam at each end, sew a rectangle to each end of the center rectangle, one at a time, then cut away excess and press.

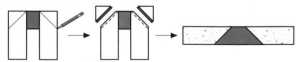

1. Following the directions for "Angled Piecing" on page 106 and referring to the illustrations below, make rows 1–4 for the star blocks.

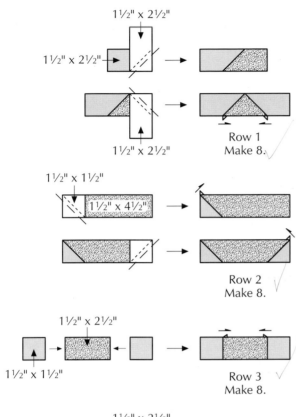

Row 1
Make 8.

Row 2
Make 8.

Row 3
Make 8.

Row 4
Make 8.

2. Arrange the units from step 1 to make 8 stars. Sew the strips together to complete each one. Each star should measure 4½" x 4½".

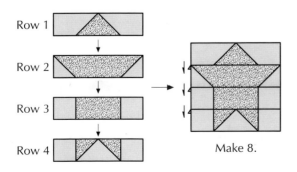

Row 1

Row 2

Row 3

Row 4

Make 8.

3. Add a 1½" x 4½" background rectangle to the top edge of 4 stars and to the bottom edge of 3 stars. Sew a 1" x 4½" rectangle to the top of the remaining star and set aside. Press the seam toward the rectangle in each star block.

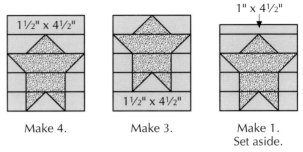

Make 4.   Make 3.   Make 1.
Set aside.

4. Arrange the 7 stars in a row as shown and sew together. Press the seams in one direction. The completed row should measure 5½" x 28½".

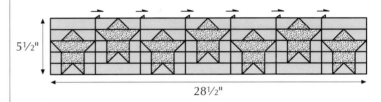

5½"

28½"

Candles

Cut all strips across the fabric width (crosswise grain) for 42"-long strips.

Fabric	No. of Strips	Strip Width	No. of Pieces	Dimensions
Background	1	1"	40	1" x 1"
	2	1½"	18	1½" x 1½"
			2	1" x 1½"
			3	1½" x 4½"
	2	2"	8	2" x 4"
			2	2" x 4½"
			2	2" x 5½"
Yellow	1	1½"	10	1½" x 1½"
Dark green	1	2"	8	2" x 2"
Assorted scraps for candles			3	1½" x 3½"
			5	1½" x 4½"
			2	1½" x 4"

1. Following the direc-
tions for "Angled Piec-
ing" on page 106, sew a
1" background square to
the upper right corner
of each yellow 1½"
square. Cut and press.
Repeat at the lower left
corner, followed by the
lower right, and finally
the upper left corner.

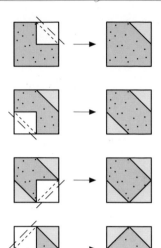

Make 10.

2. Sew a completed flame to
1 short end of each candle
(10 rectangles of assorted
prints). Press the seam toward the candle.

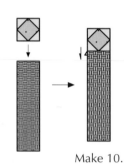

Make 10.

3. Arrange the background pieces and the pieces for
the 5 candles in the horizontal candle section and
sew together. Press the seams in the direction of
the arrows.

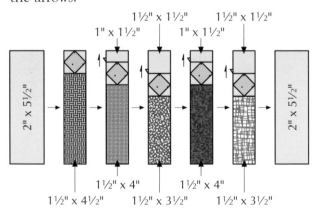

1½" x 1½"   1½" x 1½"
1" x 1½"   1" x 1½"

2" x 5½"   2" x 5½"

1½" x 4"   1½" x 4"
1½" x 4½"   1½" x 3½"   1½" x 3½"

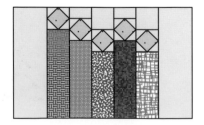

4. Following the directions for "Angled Piecing" on
page 106, sew a 1½" background square to the lower
right corner of each of the 8 dark green 2" squares.
Cut and press. Repeat at the opposite corner of
each square.

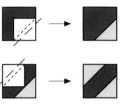

Make 8.

5. Arrange the pieces for each of 4 candle blocks and
sew together.

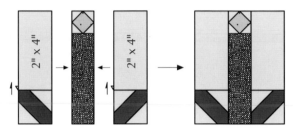

2" x 4"   2" x 4"

Make 4.

6. Sew a background strip to the top edge of 3 candles.
Press.

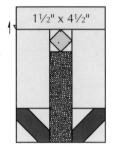

1½" x 4½"

7. Sew the candle blocks together,
adding the remaining star to the
bottom edge of the last candle. The
completed strip should measure
4½" x 28".

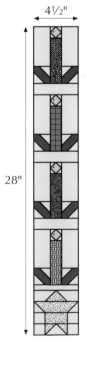

4½"

28"

8. Add a 2" x 4½" background strip to opposite sides of the remaining candle unit. Set aside for the Ohio Star block.

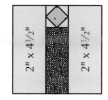

Make 1.

Ohio Star Block

Cut all strips across the fabric width (crosswise grain) for 42"-long strips.

Fabric	No. of Strips	Strip Width	No. of Pieces	Dimensions
Background	1	2½"	4	2½" x 2½"
			4	2½" x 4½"
Burgundy	1	2½"	8	2½" x 2½"

1. Following the directions for "Angled Piecing" on page 106 and using the 2½" x 4½" background pieces and the 2½" burgundy squares, make 4 star points.

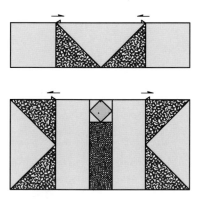

2. Add a 2½" background square to each end of 2 star points. Press the seams toward the star point. Sew a star point to opposite long sides of the remaining candle unit.

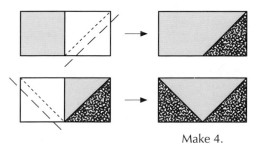

Make 4.

3. Arrange the units and sew together to complete the star section.

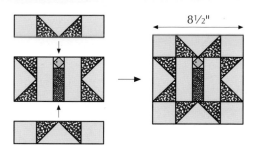

Making the Patchwork Sashing Strips

1. **From the assorted scraps, cut the following pieces:**
   4 squares, each 2½" x 2½"
   4 pieces, each 2" x 2½"
   1 piece, 2½" x 3"
   2 pieces, each 2½" x 3½"
2. Arrange the pieces in the order shown and sew together to make 2 sashing strips.

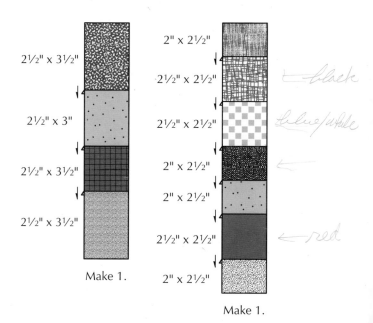

Make 1.

Make 1.

Assembling the Quilt Top

1. Cut the following pieces from the assorted light prints for the section backgrounds:
   1 piece, 2½" x 8½", for the Joy sashing strip below the horizontal row of candles
   1 strip, 11" x 14½", for the small angels section
   1 piece, 8½" x 13", for the tree section
   1 piece, 9" x 12½", for the large angel section
   1 piece, 6" x 12½", for the wreath section
   1 strip, 3½" x 16½", for the "Light a Little Candle" banner

2. Using the blue water-soluble marking pen and, referring to the quilt plan, write "Joy Joy Joy Joy" on the 2½" x 8½" sashing strip. Write "Light a Little Candle to Brighten your Spirit and Bring you Joy" on the 3½" x 16½" sashing strip. See page 112 for the lettering patterns. Using 3 strands of black embroidery floss and a backstitch, embroider over the words; take stitches through all quilt layers. Use French knots to dot the I's.

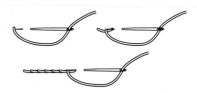

Stem Stitch

French Knot

3. From the blue print, cut 2 strips, each 1½" x 16½", for the banner borders. Sew a strip to the top and bottom edge of the 3½" x 16½" background strip for the banner. Press seams toward the blue strips.

4. Referring to the illustration below, arrange the pieced sections and background pieces and sew together as shown. Sew the larger sections together.

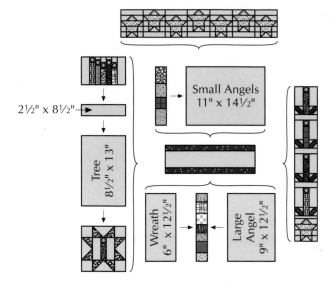

5. From burgundy print #1, cut 4 strips, each 1½" x 42", for the inner border. From these, cut 2 strips, each 1½" x 28½", and sew to the top and bottom edges of the quilt top. From the remaining strips, cut 2 strips, each 1½" x 35". Sew to opposite sides of the quilt top.

6. From the green print for the outer border, cut 4 strips, each 3½" x 42". From these, cut 2 strips, each 3½" x 30½", and sew to the top and bottom edges of the quilt top. From the remaining strips, cut 2 strips, each 3½" x 41", and sew to opposite sides of the quilt top.

Appliquéing the Pieces
Use the patterns on pages 113–17.

Note: For best results when fusing the pieces, carefully follow the manufacturer's instructions. Be sure to use the recommended heat settings; an iron that is too hot will cause the adhesive to bleed through the fabrics, and the pieces won't stick.

1. Apply fusible interfacing to the wrong side of the white and other light-colored fabrics before cutting the pieces. This will prevent dark colors from showing through the appliqués.

2. Trace each appliqué piece on the paper side of the fusible web, leaving ½" between pieces.

Note: *The appliqué pieces are drawn in reverse on the pages of this book. When you trace and apply them as directed here, they will appear as they do in the quilt photo on page 104.*

3. Cut out the pieces, leaving a 1/4"-wide seam allowance all around.

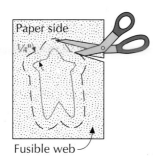

Paper side

Fusible web

4. For each appliqué, place the chosen fabric, wrong side up, on your ironing surface. Lay the fusible web, paper side up, on top. Fuse in place and allow to cool. Cut out the shape on the traced line.

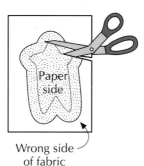

Paper side

Wrong side of fabric

5. Leave the paper backing on the larger pieces but remove the paper backing from small pieces that must be applied to larger ones (such as the stars on the apron and wings). Fuse the small pieces in place.

6. Remove the paper from the large appliqués and position them on the appropriate background. Refer to the color photo for placement and to the placement guides on pages 113–15 and 117. Fuse in place.

Note: If any of the pieces lift, turn the quilt top over and fuse from the back, or place a book on top of the fused area and apply pressure until the fabric cools.

Finishing

Refer to pages 124–28 to finish your quilt.

1. On the light-colored and gold appliqué pieces, use the black permanent marker to draw quilting "stitches," 1/16" to 1/8" long, as close to the edges as possible.

2. Mark the quilt top with the desired quilting pattern in each background area or see the quilting suggestion below.

3. Layer the quilt top with batting and backing; baste.

4. Quilt on the marked lines. Quilt 1/4" beyond the outer edges of the appliqués.

5. Add a hanging sleeve if desired.

6. Bind the edges with double-fold binding, using 2 1/2"-wide straight-grain strips cut from burgundy print #2.

7. Thread a craft needle with 3 strands of black embroidery floss; don't knot the end. Position a black button in the center of each pieced star and at random in the patchwork sashing squares. Beginning on the top of the quilt, insert the needle through 1 hole of the button to the back of the quilt, then bring up through the second hole. Clip the floss, leaving a 2" tail at each end. Tie the tails together in a knot and add a dab of white fabric glue. Trim the tails to 1/4".

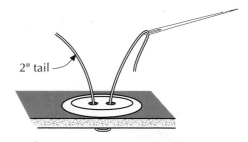

2" tail

8. Scatter the small buttons on the Christmas tree and sew in place as in step 7.
9. Draw the faces on the angels as shown at right. Using a cotton-tipped swab, place a dot of blush on the cheeks.
10. Sign your quilt.

Embroidery Templates

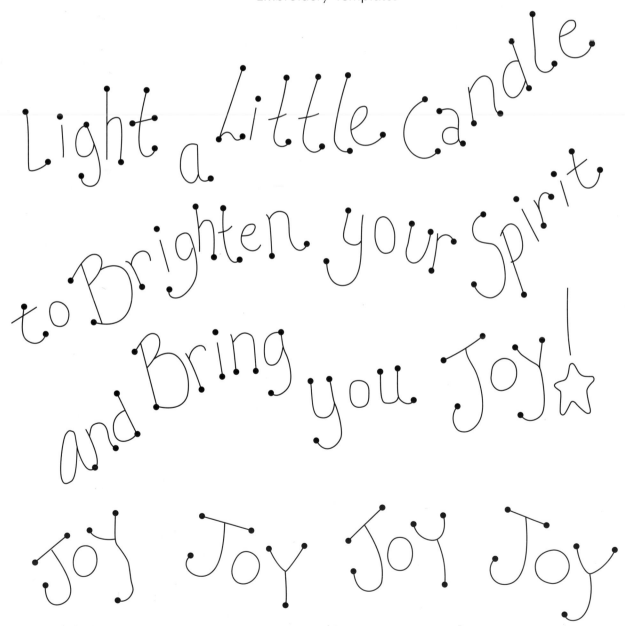

Christmas Tree
Appliqué Templates

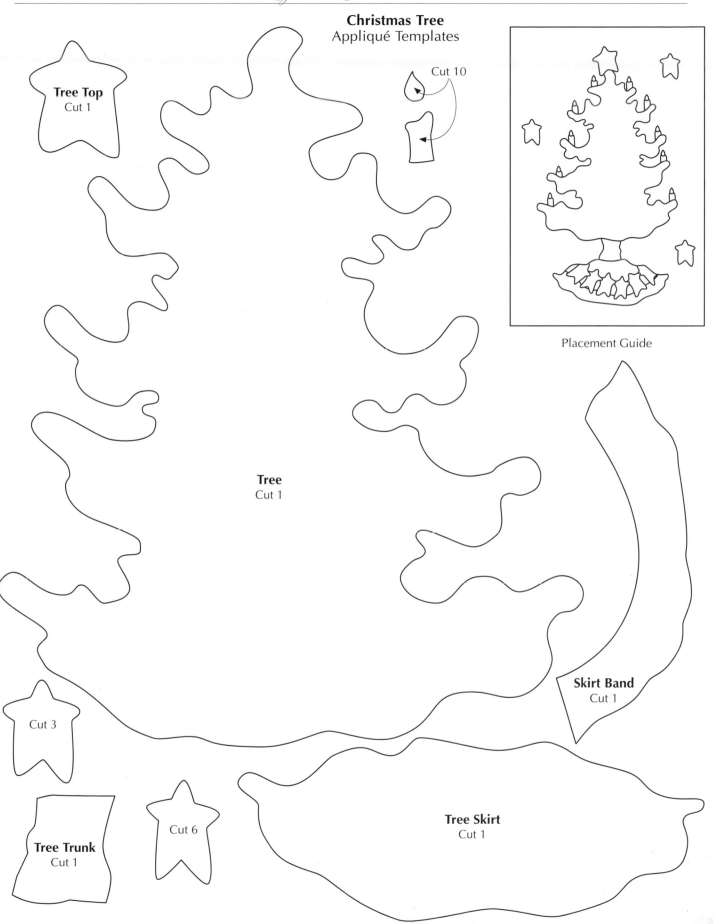

Cut 10

Tree Top
Cut 1

Placement Guide

Tree
Cut 1

Skirt Band
Cut 1

Cut 3

Tree Trunk
Cut 1

Cut 6

Tree Skirt
Cut 1

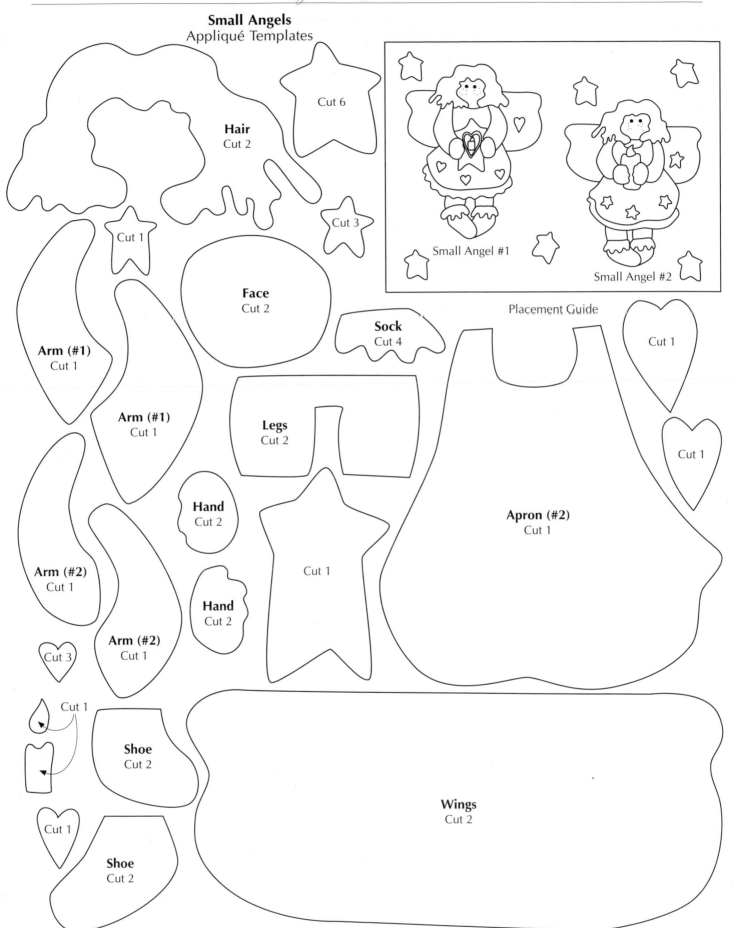

Small Angels
Appliqué Templates

Cut 6

Hair
Cut 2

Cut 1

Cut 3

Small Angel #1

Small Angel #2

Placement Guide

Face
Cut 2

Sock
Cut 4

Cut 1

Arm (#1)
Cut 1

Arm (#1)
Cut 1

Legs
Cut 2

Cut 1

Cut 1

Hand
Cut 2

Apron (#2)
Cut 1

Arm (#2)
Cut 1

Hand
Cut 2

Cut 1

Cut 3

Arm (#2)
Cut 1

Cut 1

Shoe
Cut 2

Cut 1

Wings
Cut 2

Shoe
Cut 2

Small Angels/Wreath
Appliqué Templates

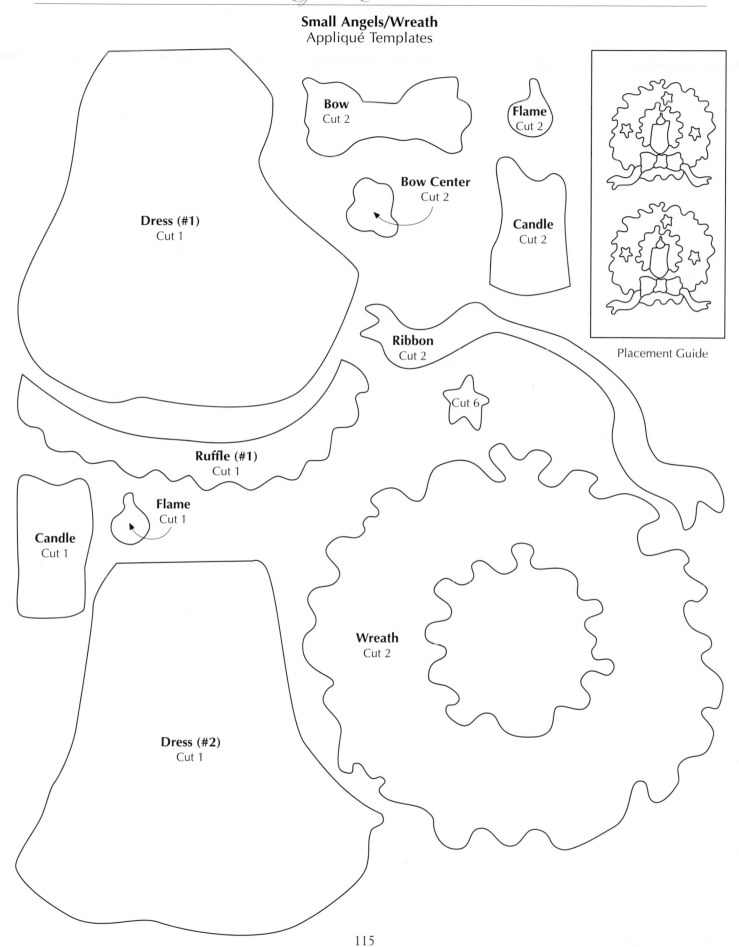

Bow
Cut 2

Flame
Cut 2

Bow Center
Cut 2

Candle
Cut 2

Dress (#1)
Cut 1

Ribbon
Cut 2

Cut 6

Ruffle (#1)
Cut 1

Candle
Cut 1

Flame
Cut 1

Dress (#2)
Cut 1

Wreath
Cut 2

Placement Guide

115

Large Angel
Appliqué Templates

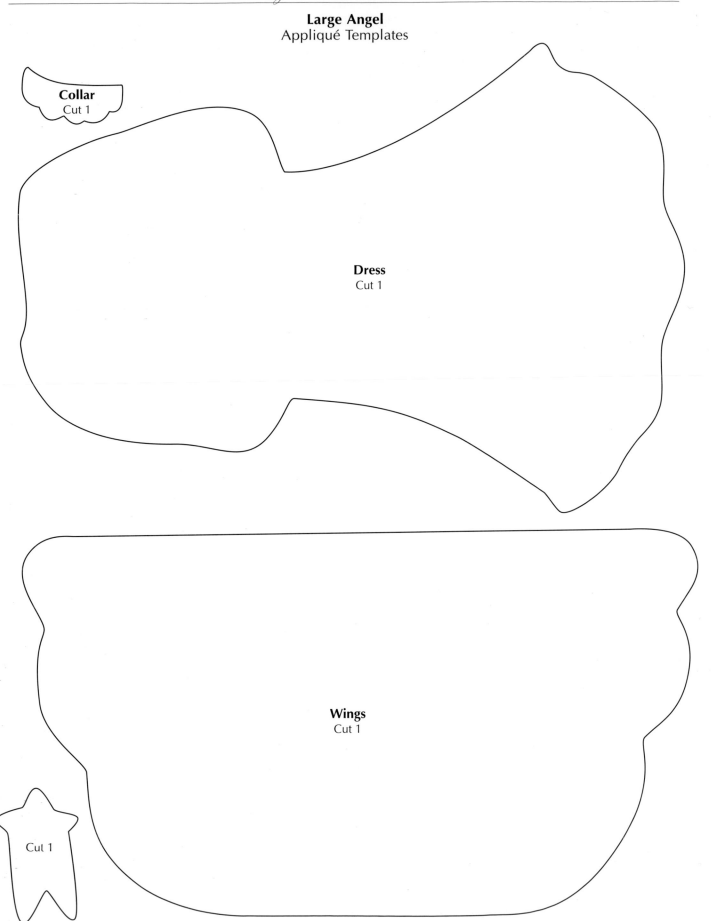

Collar
Cut 1

Dress
Cut 1

Wings
Cut 1

Cut 1

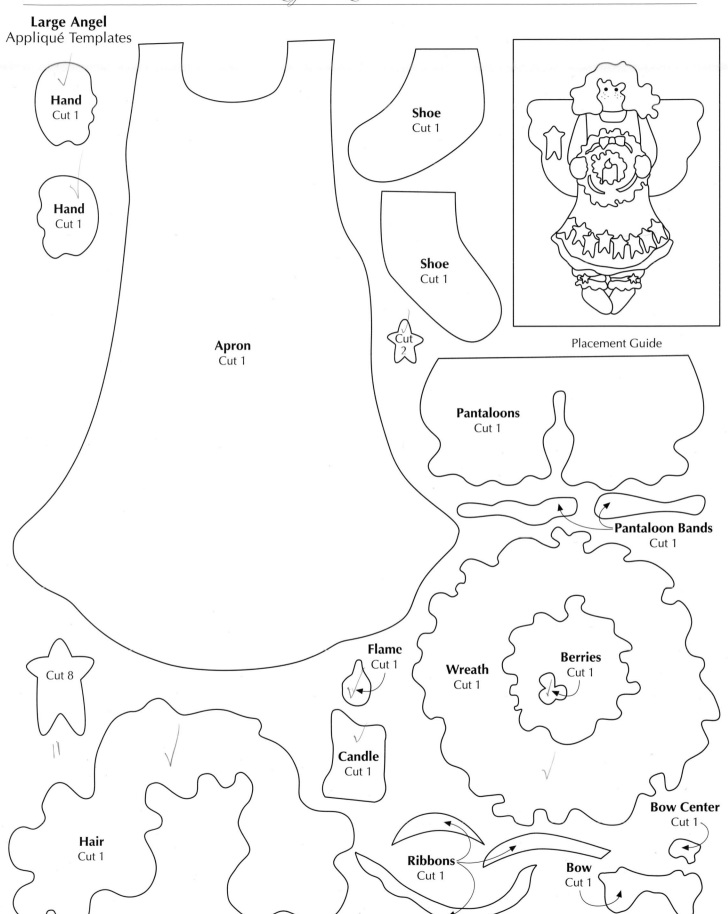

Large Angel
Appliqué Templates

Hand
Cut 1

Hand
Cut 1

Apron
Cut 1

Shoe
Cut 1

Shoe
Cut 1

Cut 2

Placement Guide

Pantaloons
Cut 1

Pantaloon Bands
Cut 1

Cut 8

Flame
Cut 1

Wreath
Cut 1

Berries
Cut 1

Candle
Cut 1

Bow Center
Cut 1

Hair
Cut 1

Ribbons
Cut 1

Bow
Cut 1

117

Quiltmaking Basics

FABRIC

Select high-quality, 100% cotton fabrics. They hold their shape well and are easy to handle. Cotton blends can be more difficult to stitch and press. Sometimes, however, a cotton blend or other special fabric is worth a little extra effort if it is the perfect fabric for your quilt.

Yardage requirements are provided for all the projects in this book and are based on 42" of usable fabric after preshrinking. Some quilts call for an assortment of scraps. If you have access to scraps, feel free to use them and purchase only those fabrics you need to complete the quilt you are making.

Preshrink all fabric to test for colorfastness and remove excess dye. Wash dark and light colors separately so that dark colors do not run onto light fabrics. Some fabrics may require several rinses to eliminate the excess dyes. Iron fabrics so that you can cut out the pieces accurately.

SUPPLIES

Sewing Machine: To machine piece, you'll need a sewing machine that has a good straight stitch. You'll also need a walking foot or darning foot if you are going to machine quilt.

Rotary-Cutting Tools: You will need a rotary cutter, cutting mat, and clear acrylic rulers in a variety of sizes, including 6" x 24" and 12" x 12". A Bias Square® ruler is helpful for cutting bias squares.

Thread: Use a good-quality, all-purpose cotton or cotton-covered polyester thread.

Needles: For machine piecing, a size 10/70 or 12/80 works well for most cottons.

For hand appliqué, choose a needle that will glide easily through the edges of the appliqué pieces. Size 10 (fine) to size 12 (very fine) needles work well.

Pins: Long, fine "quilters' pins" with glass or plastic heads are easy to handle. Small 1/2"- to 3/4"-long sequin pins work well for appliqué.

Scissors: Use your best scissors to cut fabric only. Use an older pair of scissors to cut paper, cardboard, and template plastic. Small, 4" scissors with sharp points are handy for clipping thread.

Sandpaper Board: This is an invaluable tool for accurately marking fabric. You can easily make one by adhering very fine sandpaper to a hard surface, such as wood, cardboard, poster board, or needlework mounting board. The sandpaper grabs the fabric and keeps it from slipping as you mark.

Template Plastic: Use clear or frosted plastic (available at quilt shops) to make durable, accurate templates.

Seam Ripper: Use this tool to remove stitches from incorrectly sewn seams.

Marking Tools: A variety of tools are available to mark fabrics when tracing around templates or marking quilting lines. Use a sharp No. 2 pencil or fine-lead mechanical pencil on lighter-colored fabrics, and a silver or yellow marking pencil on darker fabrics. Chalk pencils or chalk-wheel markers also make clear marks on fabric. Be sure to test your marking tool to make sure you can remove the marks easily.

ROTARY CUTTING

Instructions for quick-and-easy rotary cutting are provided wherever possible. All measurements include standard 1/4"-wide seam allowances. For those unfamiliar with rotary cutting, a brief introduction is provided below. For more detailed information, see Donna Thomas's *Shortcuts: A Concise Guide to Rotary Cutting* (That Patchwork Place).

1. Fold the fabric and match selvages, aligning the crosswise and lengthwise grains as much as possible. Place the folded edge closest to you on the cutting mat. Align a square ruler along the folded edge of the fabric. Then place a long, straight ruler to the left of the square ruler, just covering the uneven raw edges of the left side of the fabric.

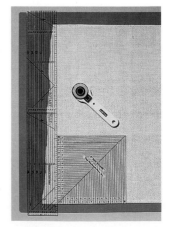

Remove the square ruler and cut along the right edge of the long ruler, rolling the rotary cutter away from you. Discard this strip. (Reverse this procedure if you are left-handed.)

2. To cut strips, align the required measurement on the ruler with the newly cut edge of the fabric. For example, to cut a 3"-wide strip, place the 3" ruler mark on the edge of the fabric.

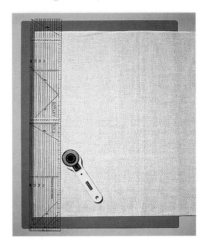

3. To cut squares, cut strips in the required widths. Trim away the selvage ends of the strip. Align the required measurement on the ruler with the left edge of the strip and cut a square. Continue cutting squares until you have the number needed.

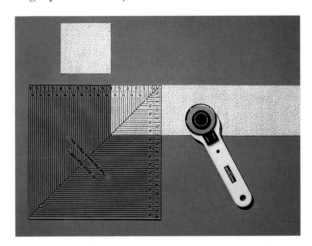

4. Cut squares in half once diagonally for half-square triangles. For quarter-square triangles, cut squares in half twice diagonally.

Half-Square   Quarter-Square
Triangle   Triangle

MACHINE PIECING
Making Templates

Most blocks are designed for easy rotary cutting and quick piecing. Some blocks, however, require the use of templates for particular shapes. Templates for machine piecing include the required $\frac{1}{4}$"-wide seam allowances. Cut out the template on the outside line so that it includes the seam allowances. Be sure to mark the pattern name and grain-line arrow on the template.

Seam Allowances

The most important thing to remember about machine piecing is to maintain a consistent $\frac{1}{4}$"-wide seam allowance. Otherwise, the quilt block will not be the desired finished size. If that happens, the size of everything else in the quilt is affected, including alternate blocks, sashings, and borders. Measurements for all components of each quilt are based on blocks that finish accurately to the desired size plus $\frac{1}{4}$" on each edge for seam allowances.

Take the time to establish an exact $\frac{1}{4}$"-wide seam guide on your machine. Some machines have a special quilting foot that measures exactly $\frac{1}{4}$" from the center needle position to the edge of the foot. This feature allows you to use the edge of the presser foot to guide the fabric for a perfect $\frac{1}{4}$"-wide seam allowance.

If your machine doesn't have such a foot, create a seam guide by placing the edge of a piece of tape, moleskin, or a magnetic seam guide $\frac{1}{4}$" away from the needle.

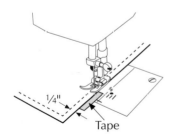

$\frac{1}{4}$"   Tape

Chain Piecing

Chain piecing is an efficient system that saves time and thread.

1. Sew the first pair of pieces from cut edge to cut edge, using 12 to 15 stitches per inch. At the end of the seam, stop sewing but *do not* cut the thread.

2. Feed the next pair of pieces under the presser foot, as close as possible to the first pair. Continue feeding pieces through the machine without cutting the threads in between. There is no need to backstitch, since each seam will be crossed by another seam.

3. When all pieces have been sewn, re-move the chain from the machine and clip the threads between the pieces.

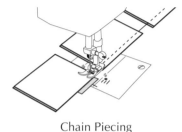

Chain Piecing

Easing

If two pieces being sewn together are slightly different in size (less than $1/8$"), pin the places where the two pieces *should* match, and in the middle if necessary, to distribute the excess fabric evenly. Sew the seam with the longer piece on the bottom. The feed dogs will ease the two pieces together.

←Excess

Pressing

The traditional rule in quiltmaking is to press seams to one side, toward the darker color wherever possible. Press the seam flat from the wrong side first, then press the seam in the desired direction from the right side. Press carefully to avoid distorting the shapes.

When joining two seamed units, plan ahead and press the seam allowances in opposite directions as shown. This reduces bulk and makes it easier to match seam lines. Where two seams meet, the seam allowances will butt against each other, making it easier to join units with perfectly matched seam intersections.

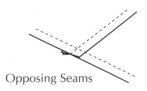

Opposing Seams

Making Bias Squares

Many quilt patterns contain squares made from two contrasting half-square triangles. These are called bias squares or half-square triangle units. There are several different methods for making these units.

Using the bias strip–piecing method is especially useful for making large numbers of bias squares. This method is very accurate because seams are pressed after strips are pieced and before squares are cut. Instructions follow for making bias squares using Mary Hickey's method, as first shown in her book *Angle Antics* (That Patchwork Place).

An alternate method, cut-and-pieced squares, can be used when you need only a small number of units, or you need units in several different combinations. This method, which is explained on page 121, requires careful pressing after squares are stitched and cut.

Bias Strip–Piecing Method

You will need a Bias Square ruler to cut the units.

1. Layer the two fabrics with right sides facing up.

2. Establish a true bias line on the top fabric, using a ruler with a 45°-angle line. Cut bias strips parallel to the drawn line. Each quilt plan will specify how wide to cut the bias strips.

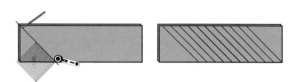

3. Sew the full-length bias strips together along the bias edges, offsetting the tops of the strips $1/4$" as shown. Alternating the fabrics, sew the strips into units of six to eight strips. Press seams toward the darker strips. When making $1 1/2$" or smaller bias squares, press seams open to distribute the bulk.

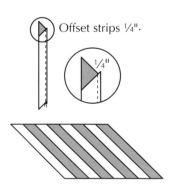

Offset strips $1/4$".

$1/4$"

4. Position the Bias Square with the diagonal line on a seam line. Place a long ruler across the top to cut an even edge. The trimmed edge should be at a perfect 45° angle to the seam lines.

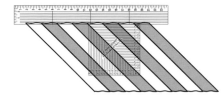

5. Cut a segment parallel to the first cut. Each quilt plan will specify how wide to cut this segment. Continue cutting segments into the specified widths, making sure to check and correct the angle at the edge after each cut.

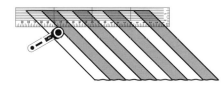

6. Sew the segments together, end to end, to create a long strip-pieced unit. This method prevents wasting triangles at the end of each unit. Be careful not to stretch the bias edges as you sew.

7. Place the Bias Square with the diagonal line on the seam line and one edge of the square on the bottom edge of the strip. Cut one side.

8. Place the diagonal line of the Bias Square on the seam line and the bottom edge of the ruler on the cut edge of the strip and cut the next bias square. The edges of the square should be lined up with the markings on the ruler to cut the required-size squares.

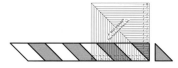

9. Continue cutting squares across the remainder of the strip until you have the number of bias squares required for the quilt you are making. Remember to align the diagonal line on the ruler with the seam line before each cut.

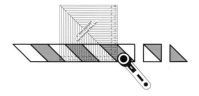

Cut-and-Pieced Squares

Remember to press carefully to avoid distorting the half-square triangle units.

1. Cut squares the size instructed in the quilt plan.
2. Draw a diagonal line from corner to corner on the back of the lightest fabric.
3. Place the square with the drawn line on top of another square, with right sides together. Sew ¼" away from the drawn line on both sides.

4. Cut on the drawn line. Press the seams toward the darker fabric and trim the "dog-ear" corners. Each pair of squares you sew together yields two half-square triangle units.

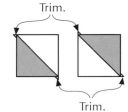

Trim.

Trim.

BASIC APPLIQUÉ

Instructions are provided for three different appliqué methods. Choose one of the following or use your own favorite method.

Making Templates

Templates made from clear plastic are more durable and accurate than those made from cardboard. Since you can see through the plastic, it is easy to trace the templates accurately.

Place template plastic over each pattern piece and trace with a fine-line permanent marker. Do not add seam allowances. Cut out the templates on the drawn lines. You need only one template for each different design. Mark the pattern name and grain-line arrow (if applicable) on the template.

Marking and Cutting Fabric

Place the template right side up on the right side of the appliqué fabric. Leave at least ½" between tracings if several pieces are needed. Cut out each fabric piece, adding a scant ¼"-wide seam allowance around each tracing. This seam allowance will be turned under to create the finished edge of the appliqué. On very small pieces, you may wish to add only ⅛" for easier handling.

The background fabric is usually a rectangle or square. Cut fabric the size and shape required for each project. It is better to cut the background an inch larger than needed in each direction to start, then trim it to the correct size after the appliqué has been sewn in place on the background fabric.

Place the background square or rectangle right side up over the pattern so that the design is centered. Lightly trace the design with a pencil. If your background fabric is dark, use a light box, or try taping the pattern to a window or storm door on a sunny day.

Traditional Appliqué Method

Before sewing appliqué pieces to the background, turn under the seam allowance, rolling the traced line to the back. Baste around each piece. Try looking at the right side of the piece while you turn the edge under, basting right along the fold. This helps to keep the piece neat and accurate as you concentrate on the smooth shape of the piece. If you keep your stitches near the fold, you will be sure to catch the seam allowance.

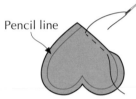

Pencil line

Do not turn under edges that will be covered by other appliqué pieces. They should lie flat under the covering appliqué piece.

Raw edge

Pin or baste the appliqué pieces to the background fabric. If you have trouble with threads tangling around pins as you sew, try placing the pins on the underside of your work.

Traditional Appliqué Stitch

The traditional appliqué stitch or blind stitch is appropriate for sewing all appliqué shapes, including sharp points and curves.

1. Tie a knot in a single strand of thread that is approximately 18" long.
2. Hide the knot by slipping the needle into the seam allowance from the wrong side of the appliqué piece, bringing it out on the fold line.
3. Work from right to left if you are right-handed, or left to right if you are left-handed.
4. Start the first stitch by moving the needle straight off the appliqué, inserting the needle into the background fabric. Let the needle travel under the background fabric, parallel to the edge of the appliqué; bring it up about ⅛" away, along the pattern line.

5. As you bring the needle up, pierce the edge of the appliqué piece, catching only one or two threads of the folded edge.
6. Move the needle straight off the appliqué into the background fabric. Let your needle travel under the background, bringing it up about ⅛" away, again catching the edge of the appliqué.
7. Give thread a slight tug and continue stitching.

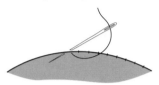

Appliqué Stitch

8. To end your stitching, pull the needle through to the wrong side. Behind the appliqué piece, take 2 small stitches, making knots by taking your needle through the loops. Check the right side to see if the thread "shadows" through your background. If it does, take 1 more small stitch on the back side to direct the tail of the thread under the appliqué fabric.

Stitching Outside Points

As you stitch toward an outside point, start taking smaller stitches within ½" of the point. Trim the seam allowance or push the excess fabric under the point with the tip of your needle. Smaller stitches near the point will keep any frayed edges from escaping.

Place the last stitch on the first side very close to the point. Place the next stitch on the second side of the point. A stitch on each side, close to the point, will accent the outside point.

Stitching Along a Curve

Push the fabric under with the tip of your needle, smoothing it out along the folded edge before sewing.

Stitching Inside Points

Make your stitches smaller as you sew within ½" of the point. Stitch past the point, then return to the point to add one extra stitch to emphasize it. Come up through the appliqué, catching a little more fabric in the inside point (four or five threads instead of one or two). Make a straight stitch outward, going under the point to pull it in a little and emphasize its shape.

If your inside point frays, use a few close stitches to tack the fabric down securely. If your thread matches your appliqué fabric, these stitches will blend in with the edge of the shape.

Alternate Appliqué Methods

Needle-Turn Appliqué

This method moves directly from cutting to the appliqué stitch. You do not turn under and baste the seam allowances.

1. Using a plastic template, trace the design onto the right side of the appliqué fabric.
2. Cut out the fabric piece, adding a scant $1/4$"-wide seam allowance all around.
3. Position the appliqué piece on the background fabric; pin or baste in place.
4. Starting on a straight edge, use the tip of the needle to gently turn under the seam allowance, about $1/2$" at a time. Hold the turned seam allowance firmly between the thumb and first finger of your left hand (reverse if left-handed) as you stitch the appliqué to the background. Use a longer needle—a Sharp or milliner's needle—to help you control the seam allowance and turn it under neatly.

Note: Stitches in illustration show placement. They should *not* show in completed work.

Pencil line

Freezer-Paper Appliqué

Use freezer paper (plastic coated on one side) to help make perfectly shaped appliqués. You can trace around a template or simply trace the design onto the freezer paper. The seam allowances are then turned over the freezer-paper edges and basted or glued to the back side before appliquéing the shape to the background.

1. Place freezer paper, plastic side down, on top of the pattern and trace the design with a sharp pencil.

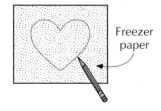

Freezer paper

2. Cut out the freezer paper design on the pencil line. Do not add seam allowances.
3. With the plastic-coated side against the wrong side of the fabric, iron the freezer paper in place, using a hot, dry iron.

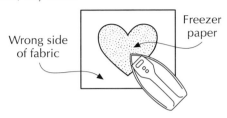

Freezer paper

Wrong side of fabric

4. Cut out the shape, adding $1/4$"-wide seam allowances all around the outside edge of the freezer paper.

5. Turn and baste the seam allowance over the freezer-paper edges by hand, or use a glue stick. (Clip inside points and fold outside points.)

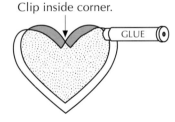

Clip inside corner.

GLUE

6. Pin or baste the design to the background fabric. Appliqué the design.
7. Remove any basting stitches. Cut a small slit in the background fabric behind the appliqué and remove the freezer paper with tweezers. If you used a glue stick, soak the piece in warm water for a few minutes before removing the freezer paper.

ASSEMBLING THE QUILT TOP
Squaring up Blocks

When your blocks are complete, take the time to square them up. Use a large square ruler to measure your blocks and make sure they are the desired size plus an extra ¼" on each edge for seam allowances. For example, if you are making 6" blocks, they should all measure 6½" before you sew them together. Trim the larger blocks to match the smallest one. Be sure to trim all four sides; otherwise your block will be lopsided.

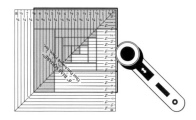

If your blocks are not the required finished size, you will have to adjust all the other components of the quilt accordingly.

Making Straight-Set Quilts

1. Arrange the blocks as shown in the quilt plan provided with each quilt.
2. Sew blocks together in horizontal rows; press the seams in opposite directions from row to row.

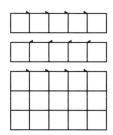

Straight-Set Quilts

3. Sew the rows together, making sure to match the seams between the blocks.

Adding Borders

For best results, do not cut border strips and sew them directly to the quilt sides without measuring first. The edges of a quilt often measure slightly longer than the distance through the quilt center, due to stretching during construction. Instead, measure the quilt top through the center in both directions to determine how long to cut the border strips. This step ensures that the finished quilt will be as straight and as "square" as possible, without wavy edges.

Plain border strips are commonly cut along the crosswise grain and seamed where extra length is needed. Borders cut from the lengthwise grain of fabric require extra yardage, but seaming the required length is then unnecessary.

You may add borders that have straight-cut corners or mitered corners. Check the quilt pattern you are following.

Straight-Cut Borders

1. Measure the length of the quilt top through the center. Cut border strips to that measurement, piecing as necessary; mark the center of the quilt edges and the border strips. Pin the borders to the sides of the quilt top, matching the center marks and ends and easing as necessary. Sew the border strips in place. Press seams toward the border.

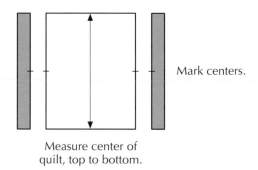

Mark centers.

Measure center of quilt, top to bottom.

2. Measure the width of the quilt top through the center, including the side borders just added. Cut border strips to that measurement, piecing as necessary; mark the center of the quilt edges and the border strips. Pin the borders to the top and bottom edges of the quilt top, matching the center marks and ends and easing as necessary; stitch. Press seams toward the border.

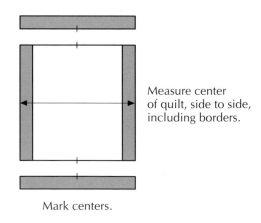

Measure center of quilt, side to side, including borders.

Mark centers.

Borders with Mitered Corners

1. First estimate the finished outside dimensions of your quilt, including borders. Border strips should be cut to this length plus at least ½" for seam allowances; it's safer to add 3" to 4" for some leeway. For example, if your quilt top measures 35½" x 50½" across the center and you want a 5"-wide finished border, your quilt will measure 45" x 60" after the borders are attached.

Note: If your quilt has multiple borders, sew the individual strips together and treat the resulting unit as a single border strip.

2. Fold the quilt in half and mark the center of the quilt edges. Fold each border strip in half and mark the center with a pin.
3. Measure the length and width of the quilt top across the center. Note the measurements.
4. Place a pin at each end of the side border strips to mark the length of the quilt top. Repeat with the top and bottom borders.

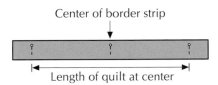

Center of border strip

Length of quilt at center

5. Pin the borders to the quilt top, matching the centers. Line up the pins at each end of the border strip with the edges of the quilt. Stitch, beginning and ending the stitching ¼" from the raw edges of the quilt top. Repeat with the remaining borders.

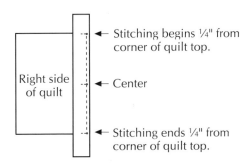

Stitching begins ¼" from corner of quilt top.

Right side of quilt

Center

Stitching ends ¼" from corner of quilt top.

6. Lay the first corner to be mitered on the ironing board. Fold under one border strip at a 45° angle to the other strip. Press and pin.

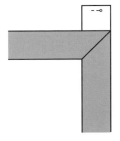

7. Fold the quilt with right sides together, lining up the edges of the border. If necessary, use a ruler to draw a pencil line on the crease to make the line more visible. Stitch on the crease, sewing from the corner to the outside edge.

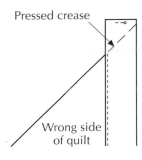

Pressed crease

Wrong side of quilt

8. Press the seam open and trim away excess border strips, leaving a ¼"-wide seam allowance.
9. Repeat with remaining corners.

PREPARING TO QUILT
Marking the Quilting Lines

Whether or not to mark the quilting designs depends upon the type of quilting you will be doing. Marking is not necessary if you plan to quilt in-the-ditch or outline quilt a uniform distance from seam lines. For more complex quilting designs, mark the quilt top before the quilt is layered with batting and backing.

Choose a marking tool that will be visible on your fabric and test it on fabric scraps to be sure the marks can be removed easily. See "Marking Tools" on page 118 for options. Masking tape can also be used to mark straight quilting. Tape only small sections at a time and remove the tape when you stop at the end of the day; otherwise, the sticky residue may be difficult to remove from the fabric.

Layering the Quilt

The quilt "sandwich" consists of backing, batting, and the quilt top.

Cut the quilt backing at least 4" larger than the quilt top all the way around. For large quilts, it is usually necessary to sew two or three lengths of fabric together to make a backing of the required size. Trim away the selvages before piecing the lengths together. Press the backing seams open to make quilting easier.

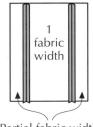

Two lengths of fabric seamed in the center

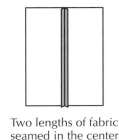

1 fabric width

Partial fabric width

Batting comes packaged in standard bed sizes, or it can be purchased by the yard. Several weights or thicknesses are available. Thick battings are fine for tied quilts and comforters; a thinner batting is better, however, if you intend to quilt by hand or machine.

To put it all together:

1. Spread the backing, wrong side up, on a flat, clean surface. Anchor it with pins or masking tape. Be careful not to stretch the backing out of shape.
2. Spread the batting over the backing, smoothing out any wrinkles.
3. Place the pressed quilt top on top of the batting. Smooth out any wrinkles and make sure the quilt-top edges are parallel to the edges of the backing.
4. Starting in the center, baste with needle and thread and work diagonally to each corner. Continue basting in a grid of horizontal and vertical lines 6" to 8" apart. Finish by basting around the edges.

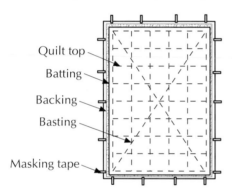

Note: For machine quilting, you may baste the layers with #2 rust-proof safety pins. Place pins about 6" to 8" apart, away from the area you intend to quilt.

QUILTING TECHNIQUES
Hand Quilting

To quilt by hand, you will need short, sturdy needles (called "Betweens"), quilting thread, and a thimble to fit the middle finger of your sewing hand. Most quilters also use a frame or hoop to support their work. Use the smallest needle you can comfortably handle; the finer the needle, the smaller your stitches will be.

1. Thread your needle with a single strand of quilting thread about 18" long; make a small knot and insert the needle in the top layer about 1" from the place where you want to start stitching. Pull the needle out at the point where quilting will begin and gently pull the thread until the knot pops through the fabric and into the batting.
2. Take small, evenly spaced stitches through all three quilt layers.

3. Rock the needle up and down through all layers, until you have three or four stitches on the needle. Place your other hand underneath the quilt so you can feel the needle point with the tip of your finger when a stitch is taken.
4. To end a line of quilting, make a small knot close to the last stitch; then, backstitch, running the thread a needle's length through the batting. Gently pull the thread until the knot pops into the batting; clip the thread at the quilt's surface.

For more information on hand quilting, refer to *Loving Stitches* by Jeana Kimball (That Patchwork Place).

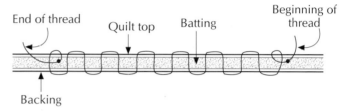

Machine Quilting

Machine quilting is suitable for all types of quilts, from crib to full-size bed quilts. With machine quilting, you can quickly complete quilts that might otherwise languish on the shelves.

Marking is only necessary if you need to follow a grid or a complex pattern. It is not necessary if you plan to quilt in-the-ditch, outline quilt a uniform distance from seam lines, or free-motion quilt in a random pattern over the quilt surface or in selected areas.

1. For straight-line quilting, it is extremely helpful to have a walking foot to help feed the quilt layers through the machine without shifting or puckering. Some machines have a built-in walking foot; other machines require a separate attachment.

Walking Foot

Quilting In-the-Ditch

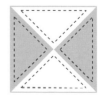

Outline Quilting

2. For free-motion quilting, you need a darning foot and the ability to drop the feed dogs on your machine. With free-motion quilting, you do not turn the fabric under the needle but instead guide the fabric in the direction of the design. Use free-motion quilting to outline-quilt a pattern in the fabric or to create stippling and many other curved designs.

Darning Foot

Free-Motion Quilting

FINISHING
Binding

Bindings can be made from straight-grain or bias-grain strips of fabric. For a French double-fold binding, cut strips 2½" wide.

Note: If you want to attach a hanging sleeve to the back of the quilt, see page 128 and make the sleeve *before* you attach the binding.

To cut straight-grain binding strips:
Cut 2½"-wide strips across the width of the fabric. You will need enough strips to go around the perimeter of the quilt plus 10" for seams and the corners in a mitered fold.

To cut bias-grain binding strips:
1. Fold a square of fabric on the diagonal.

Bias fold

OR
Fold a ½-yard piece as shown in the diagrams below, paying careful attention to the location of the lettered corners.

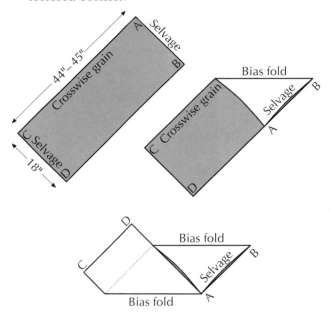

2. Cut strips 2½" wide, cutting perpendicular to the folds as shown.

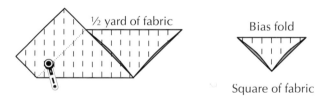

½ yard of fabric

Bias fold

Square of fabric

To attach binding:
1. Sew strips, right sides together, to make one long piece of binding. Press seams open.

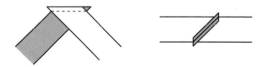

If you cut strips on the straight grain, join strips at right angles and stitch across the corner as shown. Trim excess fabric and press seams open.

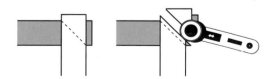

Joining Straight-Cut Strips

2. Fold the strip in half lengthwise, wrong sides together, and press.

3. Turn under ¼" at a 45° angle at one end of the strip and press. Turning the end under at an angle distributes the bulk so you won't have a lump where the two ends of the binding meet.

Fold line

4. Trim batting and backing even with the quilt top.
5. Starting on one side of the quilt and using a ⅜"-wide seam allowance, stitch the binding to the quilt, keeping the raw edges even with the quilt-top edge. End the stitching ⅜" from the corner of the quilt and backstitch. Clip the thread.

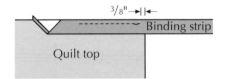

3/8"

Binding strip

Quilt top

6. Turn the quilt so you will be stitching down the next side. Fold the binding up, away from the quilt with raw edges aligned.

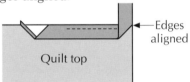

Edges aligned

Quilt top

7. Fold the binding back down onto itself, even with the edge of the quilt top. Begin stitching ⅜" from the edge, backstitching to secure.

3/8"

Quilt top

8. Repeat on the remaining edges and corners of the quilt. When you reach the beginning of the binding, overlap the beginning stitches by about 1" and cut away any excess binding, trimming the end at a 45° angle. Tuck the end of the binding into the fold and finish the seam.

Quilt top

9. Fold the binding over the raw edges of the quilt to the back, with the folded edge covering the row of machine stitching, and blindstitch in place. A miter will form at each corner. Blindstitch the mitered corners in place.

Quilt back   Quilt back

Adding a Sleeve

If you plan to display your finished quilt on the wall, be sure to add a hanging sleeve to hold the rod. When you use the following method, the top edge of the sleeve is caught in the binding seam.

1. Using leftover fabric from the front or a piece of muslin, cut a strip 6" to 8" wide and 1" shorter than the width of the quilt at the top edge. Fold the ends under ½", then ½" again, and stitch.

2. Fold the fabric strip in half lengthwise, wrong sides together. Baste the raw edges to the top edge of the back of your quilt.

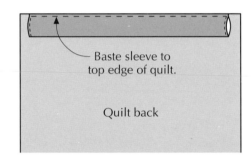

Baste sleeve to top edge of quilt.

Quilt back

3. Finish the sleeve after the binding has been attached by blindstitching the bottom of the sleeve in place. Push the bottom edge of the sleeve up just a bit to provide a little give so the hanging rod does not put strain on the quilt itself.

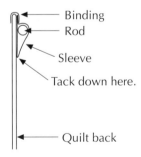

Binding
Rod
Sleeve
Tack down here.

Quilt back

Signing Your Quilt

Be sure to sign and date your quilt. Future generations will be interested to know more than just who made it and when. Labels can be as elaborate or as simple as you desire. The information can be handwritten, typed, or embroidered. Be sure to include the name of the quilt, your name, your city and state, the date, the name of the recipient if it is a gift, and any other interesting or important information about the quilt.

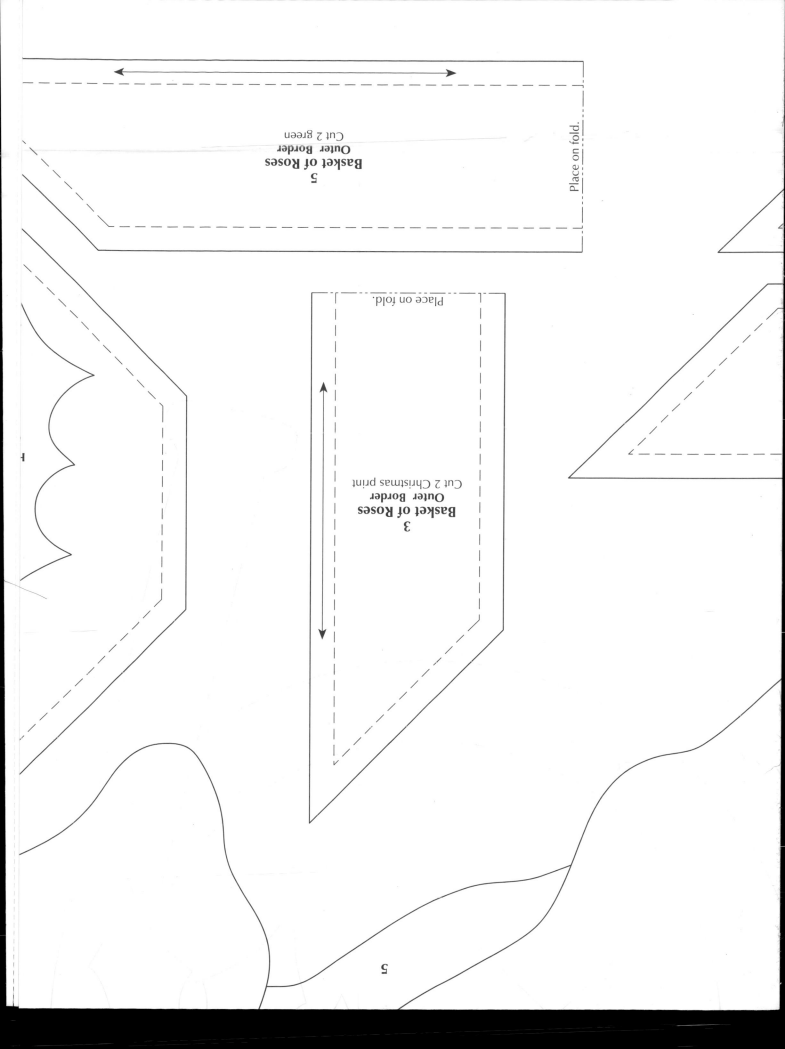

5

Basket of Roses
Outer Border
Cut 2 green

Place on fold.

3

Basket of Roses
Outer Border
Cut 2 Christmas print

Place on fold.

5

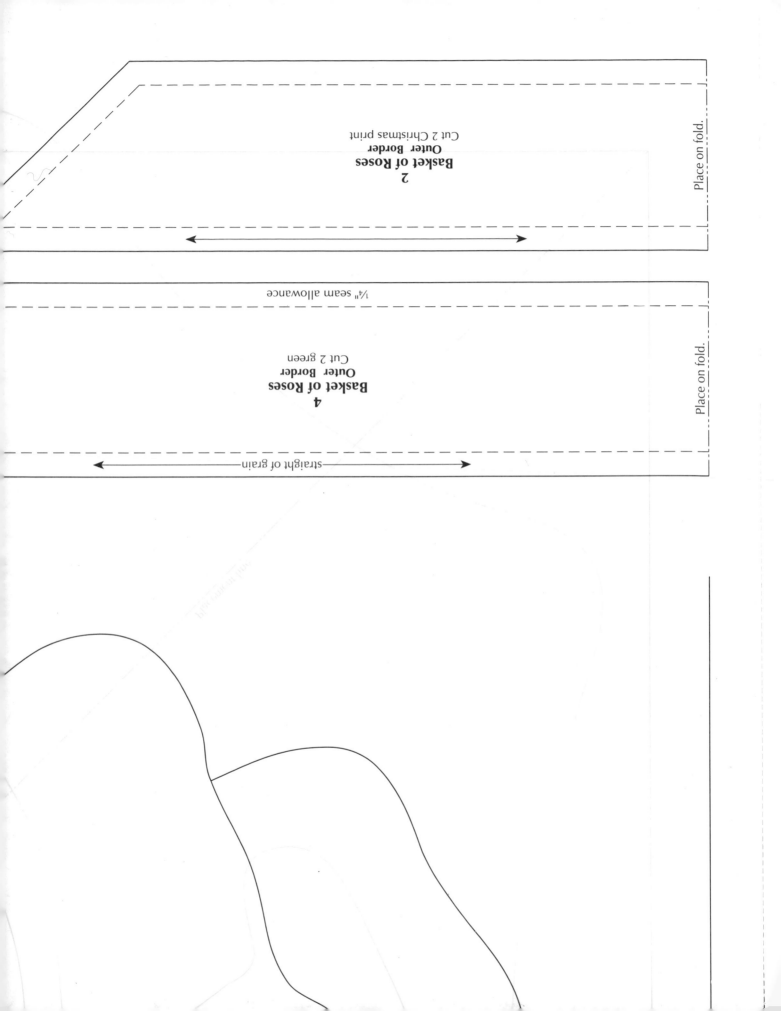

2
Basket of Roses
Outer Border
Cut 2 Christmas print

Place on fold.

¼" seam allowance

4
Basket of Roses
Outer Border
Cut 2 green

Place on fold.

straight of grain